First Edition

triumph**learning**™
Common Core Coach
English Language Arts 3

Common Core Coach, English Language Arts, First Edition, Grade 3   T102NA   ISBN-13: 978-1-61997-430-2
Cover Design: Q2A/Bill Smith   **Cover Illustration:** Jennifer Kalis

Triumph Learning® 136 Madison Avenue, 7th Floor, New York, NY 10016

Contents

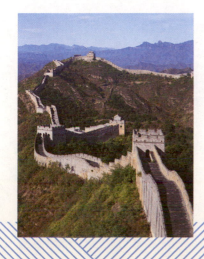

RF.3.3.c; W.3.2.a–d; W.3.4;
W.3.5; W.3.6; W.3.7; W.3.8;
W.3.10; SL.3.1.a–d; L.3.1.h, i;
L.3.2.g; L.3.3; L.3.4.d;
L.3.5.a, c

RI.3.1; RI.3.2; RI.3.3; RI.3.4;
RI.3.5; RI.3.7; RI.3.8; RI.3.10;
RF.3.4.a, c; SL.3.1.a–d; L.3.3;
L.3.4.a

W.3.1.a–d; W.3.4; W.3.5;
W.3.6; W.3.10; SL.3.1.a–d;
L.3.1.g; L.3.2.a–d; L.3.3;
L.3.5.b, c

Reading Myths and Fables

Look at this picture of the night sky.

What do you think people thought about the moon before scientists explained it?

ESSENTIAL QUESTION

How can made-up stories with imaginary characters teach important things about real life?

FABLE A fable is a story that teaches a lesson. It features animals or things in nature that behave like people. Fables are imaginary, but they include things that are true to life. This story begins with an imaginary argument between the Wind and the Sun. In what way is their argument true to life?

ASKING AND ANSWERING QUESTIONS Asking yourself questions and looking for the answers as you read can help you understand a story better. On this page you might ask, "What are the Wind and the Sun arguing about?" What other questions could you ask yourself about what is happening or what the characters are like? Look for answers to those questions as you read further.

CONTEXT CLUES You can often figure out a word you don't know by looking for hints, or context clues, in the words around it. Look at the word *defeated* in paragraph 8. What context clues can you find that help you understand the meaning of *defeated*?

What happens when two forces of nature—the Wind and the Sun—get into an argument?

In what ways are the Wind and the Sun like real people?

The Wind and the Sun

adapted from a fable by Aesop

1   One day the Wind and the Sun were arguing over which of the two was stronger.

"I'm a lot stronger than you," said the Sun.

"Don't be silly," said the Wind. "I'm truly more powerful!"

The friends argued but could not agree. Suddenly, a man wearing a dark cape came walking down the road.

5   "Here's how we can end our quarrel," the Sun said. "The one of us who can make that man take off his cape is the stronger. You go first." Then the Sun hid behind a cloud.

"That's easy," said the Wind. "I've blown hats off many people."

The Wind whipped itself up and blew against the man. This made the traveler grip his cape. The Wind decided to blow even harder, but then the man held his cape more tightly.

Finally, the Wind gave up. "I've puffed with all my might," he said in a defeated voice. "I'm all out of breath."

"It's not so easy, is it?" asked the Sun with a chuckle. "Now it's my turn."

10   The Sun beamed a few rays on the man, and he opened his cape. When the man stopped at a river for a drink, the Sun shone the full power of its heat. Soon the man was dripping with sweat. At last, he took off the cape and tossed it on the grass.

"That settles it. I'm stronger! I have won our argument," said the Sun. Then, more meekly, the Sun asked, "Can we still be friends?"

Moral: A gentle way often succeeds where a forceful way fails.

ILLUSTRATIONS
Illustrations, or pictures, can often help tell a story. A picture can show more details about the characters and help you understand them better. What do you learn about the Wind and the Sun in this picture?

MORAL "The Wind and the Sun" is a fable. It ends with a moral, or a short lesson about life. What lesson does the Wind learn in this fable? How could you use this lesson in your own life?

Consider ▶ Why does the sun come and go from the sky?
Why do we have both daylight and darkness?

Daylight

adapted from a Paiute myth

MYTH A myth is a story that tells how something in nature came to be. What do you think this myth will tell about?

USING ILLUSTRATIONS Pictures can show what characters look like and how they behave. Studying a story's illustrations can help you better understand a character's personality and actions. Look at the pictures of Tavu on these pages. What do the details in the pictures tell you about Tavu? How do these pictures help tell the story?

POINT OF VIEW Point of view shows who is telling the story. In this story, the narrator is telling the story. Who is the narrator of this story? Is it one of the characters or someone who is not part of the story? How do you know?

1 A long time ago, there were not many hours of daylight. Nights were long, and days were very short. The Paiute people did not have enough time to hunt before it got dark.

The rabbit Tavu wanted to help them, so he decided to go to the place where daylight began. He packed up his bow and his arrows and set out on a journey east toward the sun.

Tavu traveled far. He wandered through forests and hopped on stones to cross rivers. At last he came to the edge of the world, where the sun lived. He hid behind a large rock that night and waited for the sun to come out in the morning.

As soon as the sun began to rise, Tavu raised his bow and an arrow. He took aim and shot. The arrow did not get near the sun at all. It burned up before it got close. Tavu tried again. He walked closer to the sun, shooting arrows as he went. Every arrow burst into flames before it reached its mark.

5 Finally, there were only two arrows left. Tavu was upset. He sat on the ground and began to weep. He cried so much that his tears soaked his last two arrows.

Tavu gathered his strength. He took aim again and shot one of his last two arrows. He smiled when he saw how close the arrow came. It almost hit the sun! Wet with tears, the arrow did not burn up. He let his last arrow fly. This time, it struck the target. The sun fell to the ground.

Tavu moved quickly. He cut the sun into pieces and threw one piece into the sky.

"Go higher than before and make the days longer," he commanded. Then he ran away as fast as he could.

The angry sun tried to chase Tavu. Every time it came close, the clever rabbit hid. At last the sun gave up. Tavu watched it rise higher and higher into the sky. He was very pleased.

10

"Now the day will be longer," he said.

When Tavu returned, the Paiute people cheered. They held a sun dance in his honor. They begged Tavu to go fight the sun again.

"We want daylight all the time," they cheered.

"No," said Tavu. "You need night as well as day. You must have time for sleep."

And from that day to this, the world has had both daylight and darkness so that people have time to work and to rest.

DETAILS Details give information. They tell who, what, when, where, and how. One detail in the story is that Tavu's arrows got wet when he cried. Why is the wet arrow able to hit the sun?

RETELLING One way to enjoy a story is to retell it, or tell it again in your own words. To retell this story, first think about the main idea: Tavu the rabbit makes the sun stay up longer so people will have more daylight. Then think about the details that show how Tavu does this. What details would be important to include when retelling the story?

THEME This myth explains that in most parts of the world, the day is divided fairly equally into daylight and darkness. The story also has a theme. A theme is the message or truth about life that a story suggests. One theme of this story is that a small person can make a big difference, if the person is brave and determined. How do Tavu's actions in the story support this theme?

Comprehension Check

Look back at "The Wind and the Sun" and "Daylight." Fill in the chart to answer questions about each story.

	"The Wind and the Sun"	"Daylight"
Type of Story Is this story a myth or a fable?		
Characters in the Story Who are the characters in the story?		
Purpose of the Story What is the purpose of the story?		

Vocabulary

Use the word map below to help you define and use one of the highlighted vocabulary words from the Share and Learn reading or another word your teacher assigns you.

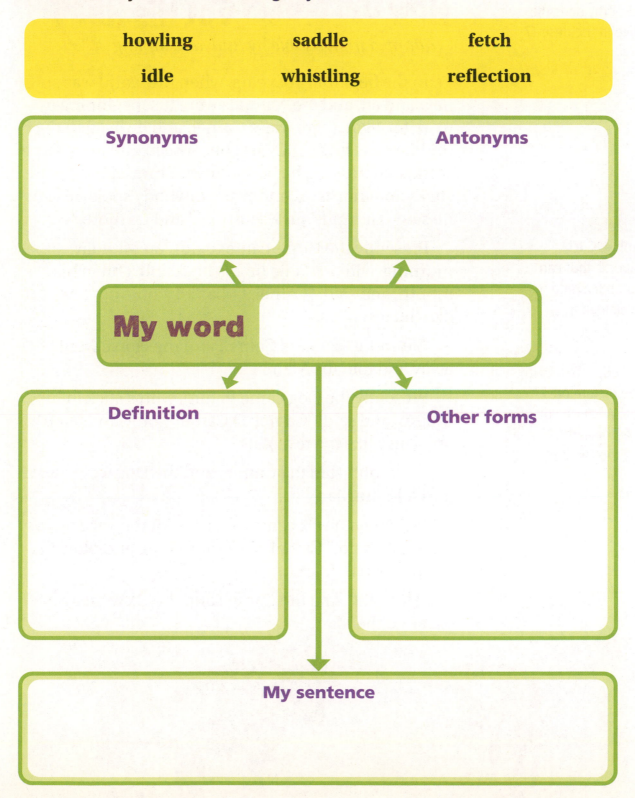

howling   saddle   fetch

idle   whistling   reflection

Synonyms

Antonyms

My word

Definition

Other forms

My sentence

Consider ▶ How do different animals work for Man in this story?

Why is the camel so well suited to living in the desert?

How the Camel Got His Hump
adapted from a fable by Rudyard Kipling

DETAILS Why does the Camel live in the desert?

_____

_____

_____

CONTEXT CLUES Find the word fetch in paragraph 4. Circle nearby words that can help you understand what *fetch* means.

USING ILLUSTRATIONS Study the picture on this page. What do you think the Horse, the Dog, and the Ox think of the Camel?

_____

_____

_____

1   In the beginning of years, when the world was so new and all, and the Animals were just beginning to work for Man, there was a Camel, and he lived in the middle of a Howling Desert because he did not want to work; and besides, he was a Howler himself. So he ate sticks and thorns . . . and when anybody spoke to him he said "Humph!" Just "Humph!" and no more.

Presently the Horse came to him on Monday morning, with a saddle on his back and a bit in his mouth, and said, "Camel, O Camel, come out and trot like the rest of us."

"Humph!" said the Camel; and the Horse went away and told the Man.

Presently the Dog came to him, with a stick in his mouth, and said, "Camel, O Camel, come and fetch and carry like the rest of us."

5   "Humph!" said the Camel; and the Dog went away and told the Man.

Presently the Ox came to him, with the yoke on his neck, and said, "Camel, O Camel, come and plow like the rest of us."

"Humph!" said the Camel; and the Ox went away and told the Man.

POINT OF VIEW Is this fable told by a story character or by a narrator who is outside the story and knows all about the characters? Explain how you can tell.

_____

_____

_____

At the end of the day the Man called the Horse and the Dog and the Ox together, and said, "Three, O Three, I'm very sorry (with the world so new-and-all); but that Humph-thing in the Desert can't work, or he would have been here by now, so I am going to leave him alone, and you must work double-time to make up for it."

That made the Three very angry (with the world so new-and-all) . . . and the Camel came chewing on milkweed *most* 'scruciatingly idle, and laughed at them. Then he said "Humph!" and went away again.

10   Presently there came along the Djinn[1] in charge of All Deserts, rolling in a cloud of dust (Djinns always travel that way.) . . .

"Djinn of All Deserts," said the Horse, "is it right for any one to be idle, with the world so new-and-all?"

"Certainly not," said the Djinn.

[1] **Djinn** in myths, a spirit that can appear in animal or human form

ASKING AND ANSWERING QUESTIONS This story has several different characters. What questions could you ask yourself about the characters and how they act toward each other?

_____

_____

_____

DETAILS What does the Camel's refusal to work mean for the other animals?

_____

_____

_____

CONTEXT CLUES Look at the word reflection on this page. Circle nearby words that can help you understand what *reflection* means.

ASKING AND ANSWERING QUESTIONS In this story, both the Camel and the Djinn have important roles. What question could you ask yourself about the role of the Djinn in this part of the story?

"Well," said the Horse, "there's a thing in the middle of your Howling Desert (and he's a Howler himself) with a long neck and long legs, and he hasn't done a stroke of work since Monday morning. He won't trot."

"Whew!" said the Djinn, whistling, "that's my Camel, for all the gold in Arabia! What does he say about it?"

15   "He says 'Humph!'" said the Dog; "and he won't fetch and carry."

"Does he say anything else?"

"Only 'Humph!'; and he won't plow," said the Ox.

"Very good," said the Djinn. "I'll humph him if you will kindly wait a minute."

The Djinn rolled himself up in his dust-cloak, and took a bearing across the desert, and found the Camel most 'scruciatingly idle, looking at his own reflection in a pool of water.

20   "My long and bubbling friend," said the Djinn, "what's this I hear of your doing no work, with the world so new-and-all?"

"Humph!" said the Camel.

The Djinn sat down, with his chin in his hand, and began to think a Great Magic, while the Camel looked at his own reflection in the pool of water.

"You've given the Three extra work ever since Monday morning, all on account of your 'scruciating idleness," said the Djinn . . . with his chin in his hand.

"Humph!" said the Camel.

25   "I shouldn't say that again if I were you," said the Djinn; "you might say it once too often. Bubbles, I want you to work."

And the Camel said "Humph!" again; but no sooner had he said it than he saw his back, that he was so proud of, puffing up and puffing up into a great big lolloping humph.

"Do you see that?" said the Djinn. "That's your very own humph that you've brought upon your very own self by not working. Today is Thursday, and you've done no work since Monday, when the work began. Now you are going to work."

"How can I," said the Camel, "with this humph on my back?"

DETAILS Both "The Wind and the Sun" and this story have a man as one of the characters. How are these human characters the same? How are they different?

_____

_____

_____

USING ILLUSTRATIONS Look at the illustrations on this page. How do the details in these illustrations help you understand the story?

_____

_____

_____

RETELLING Think about the characters and events in this story. What details would you include in a retelling of this story?

_____

_____

_____

MORAL The moral of this story is that if you avoid work and responsibility, you will suffer the consequences. How do the Camel's actions in the story support this moral?

_____

_____

_____

"That's made a-purpose," said the Djinn, "all because you missed those three days. You will be able to work now for three days without eating, because you can live on your humph; and don't you ever say I never did anything for you. Come out of the Desert and go to the Three, and behave. Humph yourself!"

And the Camel humphed himself, humph and all, and went away to join the Three. And from that day to this the Camel always wears a humph (we call it "hump" now, not to hurt his feelings), but he has never yet caught up with the three days that he missed at the beginning of the world, and he has never yet learned how to behave.

Camels are useful because they can carry heavy loads for many miles without getting tired. However, they are often stubborn and difficult for people to manage.

The camel can go without eating for a long time because its hump stores extra fat. It can burn this fat to get energy.

Anchor Standard Discussion Questions

Discuss the following questions with your peer group. Then record your answers in the space provided.

1. Do you think the Camel's punishment was fair? Support your answer with details from the text.

_____

_____

_____

_____

_____

_____

2. Now that the Camel has a hump, how might his behavior be different? How might it be the same as it was at the beginning of time? Support your answer with details from the text.

_____

_____

_____

_____

_____

_____

Comprehension Check

1. In "How the Camel Got His Hump," the Camel often says, "Humph!" Why does he say this instead of explaining why he will not work?

_____

_____

_____

2. Compare how the Man and the Djinn deal with the Camel. Which way is better? Why?

_____

_____

_____

3. In what ways are the Djinn from the fable "How the Camel Got His Hump" and the rabbit, Tavu, from the myth "Daylight" similar? In what ways are they different?

_____

_____

_____

Read On Your Own

Read another fable, "Tiger Gets His Stripes," independently. Apply what you learned in this lesson and check your understanding.

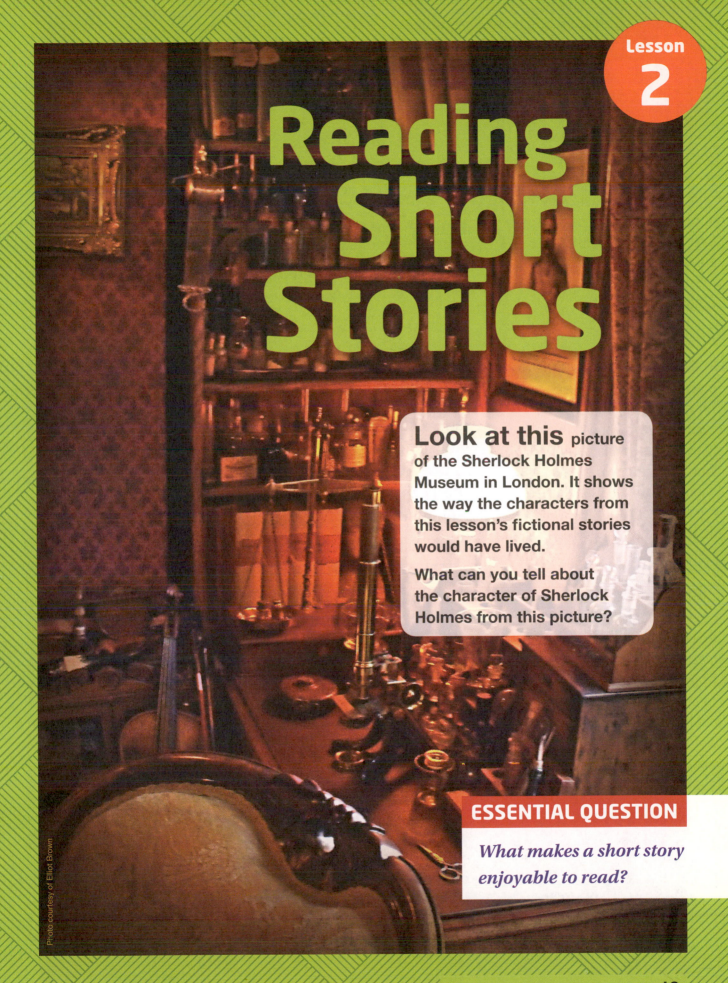

Reading Short Stories

Look at this picture of the Sherlock Holmes Museum in London. It shows the way the characters from this lesson's fictional stories would have lived.

What can you tell about the character of Sherlock Holmes from this picture?

Photo courtesy of Elliot Brown

ESSENTIAL QUESTION

What makes a short story enjoyable to read?

Consider ▶ Why do authors describe people and events in their stories in great detail?

How do authors use dialogue to describe characters?

SHORT STORIES A short story takes only a few pages to tell. Several of them may appear together in one book. Every story has a conflict, or a problem that the characters must solve. What is the problem in this story?

SEQUENCE Sequence is the order in which events happen. For a story to make sense, events have to happen in a logical order. In this story, which of these two events happens first? (a) Clark leaves the classroom. (b) The test is moved to the windowsill.

CONTEXT CLUES Context clues are words or phrases that give you clues to the meaning of an unfamiliar word. In paragraph 7, what context clues help you figure out the meaning of the word *intruder*?

The Adventure of the Three Students

adapted from the story
by Sir Arthur Conan Doyle

Chapter 1

1   Sherlock Holmes and I had left London for a few days. I always liked joining Holmes on his adventures. But for once we had no mysteries to solve. We were visiting Holmes's old college. He had some research to do at the library. We took rooms at a fine old inn. On the afternoon of the third day, we had a visit from our friend, Professor Clark. I could see that Clark was very upset.

"Holmes, Watson, you must help me," he pleaded. Clark said he had a Greek test planned for the next day. He had been in the office in his apartment all morning, preparing the test. Early that afternoon, he had left his office for a while. He had shut the office door and left the test on his desk. When he came back, the office door was open, and the test papers were on the windowsill.

"Someone came in and copied the test!" said Clark. "We must find the cheater."

We went to Clark's office.

5 "Did the thief leave any other clues?" Holmes asked.

Clark had found a small piece of black clay on his desk. Then he showed us a three-inch scratch on his desk.

"Don't worry, Clark. We'll find the intruder," said Holmes. "Could we see the room next door?"

"That's my bedroom," said Professor Clark. He led us in.

We entered Clark's bedroom. Holmes looked around. Then he saw something on the floor. "What's this?" he said.

10 Holmes held up a small piece of black clay. It was just like the clay Clark had found on his desk. "The intruder must have come in here, too," said Holmes.

"You surprised this person, Clark," continued Holmes. "That's why he didn't put the test back. He had taken it over to the office window to copy so he could watch for you coming back."

"Except I didn't pass by that window," said Clark.

ILLUSTRATIONS Pictures in a story are called illustrations. These pictures help us understand the story's characters and setting. They can add to the story's mood, or feeling, and also show us major events in the story. What is the setting of the illustration on this page? How would you describe the mood of the characters in the illustration?

SETTING The setting is where a story takes place. Unlike many other Sherlock Holmes stories, this story's setting is outside London. What details do we know about this story's setting? Why is this setting important to the plot?

CHAPTERS Chapters are sections of a story. Often, the last part of a chapter will give a clue about what comes next. Chapter 1 ends with Holmes smiling and saying he wants to meet the students. His smile is a clue to what he is thinking. What do you think will happen in the next chapter?

"Exactly. He only heard your footsteps coming. He didn't have time to put the test back on your desk. When he heard you coming, he ran in here."

"Could he have gone out the window?" I asked. We were on the first floor.

15 "Too risky, Watson," said Holmes. "Someone outside might have noticed. He must have gone out the bedroom door into the hallway. But he couldn't go back out the front door, because you would have seen him pass by your office door, Clark."

Holmes stepped out into the hallway. "What is up this stairway, Clark?"

"Well, three students live upstairs," said Clark.

"Are they all taking this test?" I asked.

"Yes," said Clark.

20 Holmes smiled. "I'd like to meet them," he said.

Chapter 2

Climbing the stairs, Holmes said, "We can't tell them our reason for visiting. We'll say that we're on a tour of the college."

On the second floor lived a student named David Martin. Clark told us he was a great athlete. Martin had won many contests in track and field, including the marathon and the long jump. He was not a top student, but Clark said he could be trusted. When we visited his room, he welcomed us in warmly. He was very friendly and quite tall.

Next we headed up to visit Rani Patel. She was a quiet young woman. She seemed slightly nervous. But she was very polite.

On the top floor lived Mark O'Brien. The professor said that he was very bright. When we knocked, O'Brien refused to let us in. "I don't care about your campus tour! I'm studying!" he yelled.

CHARACTER TRAITS
Character traits are the things that we are told about a character. These can be physical traits, such as hair color, or descriptions of the character's personality. In paragraph 22, you learn that David Martin is trustworthy, warm, friendly, and tall. What character traits does Rani Patel have?

DIALOGUE The words characters speak are called dialogue. Dialogue can help you understand a character better by showing you what he or she is like. Sherlock Holmes's dialogue in paragraph 21 shows that he is clever, always thinking and planning. What does Mark O'Brien's dialogue in paragraph 24 tell you about him?

MOTIVATIONS Motivations are the reasons characters do what they do. Sometimes characters tell us directly what their motivations are. Other times, we have to use evidence from the story to understand a character's motivation. In paragraph 24, what reason does O'Brien give when he refuses to open the door? Do you think this is his true motivation?

Holmes then asked the professor about O'Brien's height.

"Well, he's about the same height as Patel. Much shorter than Martin, of course."

Holmes then said goodnight to us both. Before leaving, he told the professor not to worry. "I'll visit in the morning. We'll find the cheat, I'm sure."

The next morning, I found Holmes at breakfast. "I have something to show you," he said proudly. In Holmes's hand, I saw three little pieces of black clay.

"I have solved the mystery, Watson."

Chapter 3

We found Clark pacing in his office. "Was it O'Brien?" he asked. "Or Miss Patel? She was as nervous as a cat when we saw her yesterday."

"Neither one," said Holmes. He then asked Clark to call Martin in. Martin entered and sat down.

Holmes spoke directly. "You are a good young man, Martin. Why would you cheat?"

Tears filled Martin's eyes. "How did you know?"

"Professor Clark said you are an expert long jumper. Yesterday, I made a visit to the school's athletic fields. In the long jump pit, I found the same clay we found in Clark's office and bedroom."

Holmes continued, "You were returning from track practice. Through the office window, you saw the test on the desk. A shorter student wouldn't have seen it. You came in and copied the test. When Professor Clark returned, you quickly grabbed your track shoes off the desk. The clay fell off your shoes. The spikes on your shoes scratched the desk, correct?"

MAKE INFERENCES

Authors do not always say everything directly. Making inferences is using details from a selection to understand things that aren't stated directly. Look at paragraph 30. The narrator says Professor Clark was pacing when he and Holmes arrived. What can we infer about Clark's mood at the time?

NONLITERAL LANGUAGE

Sometimes authors describe one thing by comparing it to another thing that's completely different. In paragraph 30, Clark says Miss Patel was "as nervous as a cat." This kind of comparison of two unlike things—Miss Patel and a cat—is an example of nonliteral language. What does Clark mean?

"Yes, sir," said Martin.

Then Martin pulled a letter out of his pocket. He handed it to Clark. "I was already going to confess. I'm terribly sorry," said Martin.

Professor Clark then said, "Martin, everyone deserves a second chance. You won't be punished. You have fallen quite low today. Let us in the future see how high you can rise."

"You have my word," said Martin.

PLOT The events in a story make up the story's plot. A plot revolves around a problem the characters must solve. The problem builds up as the story continues. The plot then reaches a turning point, or climax. This is the most exciting part of the story. Then, once the problem is solved, there is a resolution, or conclusion. Which part of the plot takes place on this page?

Comprehension Check

Look back at "The Adventure of the Three Students." How do the events of the story help you understand Sherlock Holmes's character? For each event in the chart below, explain how it helps you know what Sherlock Holmes is like.

Event: Sherlock Holmes goes to the college to do research.
Character trait: Holmes is curious and enjoys learning.

Event: Holmes agrees to help solve the mystery.

Character trait: _____

_____

_____

_____

Event: Holmes assures Clark that the cheat will be found.

Character trait: _____

_____

_____

_____

Event: Holmes explores the athletic fields.

Character trait: _____

_____

_____

_____

Vocabulary

Use the word map below to help you define and use one of the highlighted vocabulary words from the Share and Learn reading or another word your teacher assigns you.

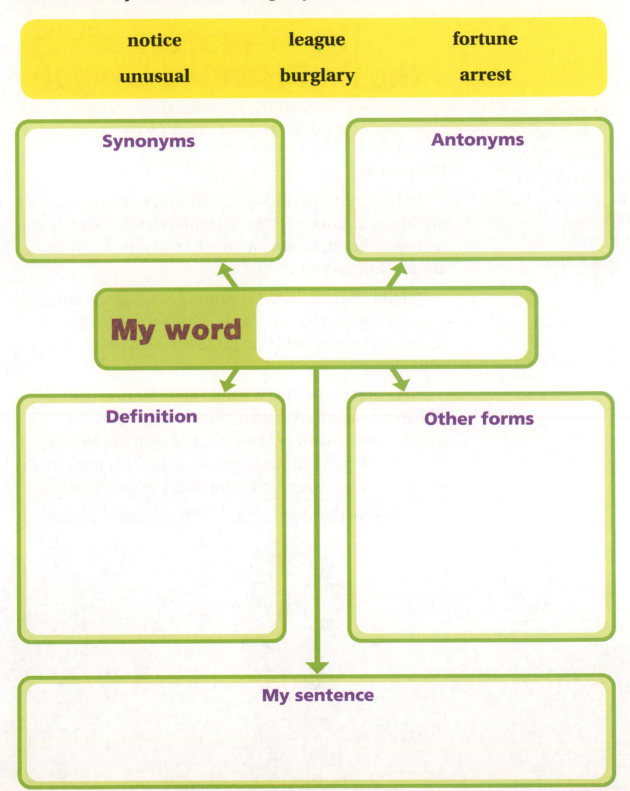

| notice | league | fortune |
| unusual | burglary | arrest |

Synonyms

Antonyms

My word

Definition

Other forms

My sentence

Consider ▶ Why do you think an author would write many books and stories about the same main character?

What do you already know about the detective Sherlock Holmes from the last story you read?

The Adventure of the Red-Headed League

*adapted from the story
by Sir Arthur Conan Doyle*

Chapter 1

ASK AND ANSWER QUESTIONS What do you want to know about the Red-Headed League? Write your question below. Keep your question in mind as you read the story.

1   It was a rainy Saturday in London. I decided to visit my friend Sherlock Holmes. I walked over to his home on Baker Street. When I arrived, I saw that Holmes already had a visitor.

"Hello, Watson," said Holmes. "Mr. Nelson here just told me an amazing story. Quite the case for us. Mr. Nelson, would you please tell Dr. Watson your story?"

"It began about two months ago," Nelson said. "I own a small bookstore. Business has been slow for a while now. One day, my clerk brought me a notice. He'd seen it in the newspaper, he said. This notice said there was a job opening in the Red-Headed League."

"The Red-Headed League? What's that?" I asked.

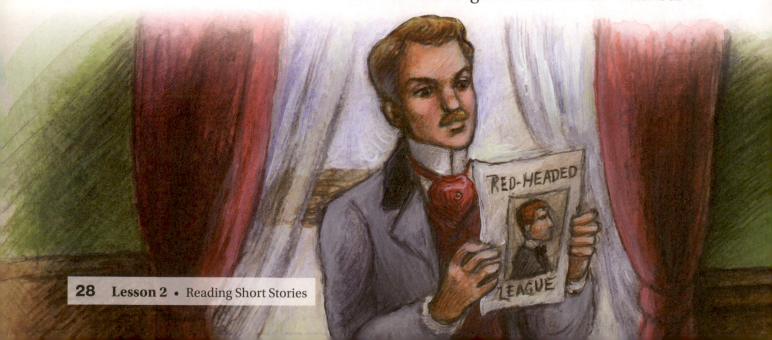

5   "I had never heard of it either," said Nelson. "A wealthy red-headed man died. He left his ==fortune== to London's red-haired people. The notice said I could make a lot of money. In return, I would not need to work much at all. It seemed too good to be true."

   Nelson pulled the notice out of his pocket. He handed it to me.

   "I thought I should find out about this group," said Nelson. "What harm could it do? I could use the money. So I decided to go to the address on the notice."

Chapter 2

   Mr. Nelson continued his story. "I couldn't believe my eyes. There was a sea of red hair outside the building. I'd never seen so many red-headed people. Finally I made my way into the office. At a small desk was a man with red hair. This fellow said I was the right one for the job. I couldn't believe it. I was hired without answering one question."

   "And what was the job?" I asked.

10   "They simply wanted me to copy every word in the dictionary. I had to show up at 10:00 every morning. If I left before 2:00, I wouldn't be paid. But why would I leave? The pay was quite good. And the work was so easy. My clerk could watch the bookshop during the mornings."

CONTEXT CLUES What words give you a clue to the meaning of the word ==fortune==? Circle them.

MOTIVATION Why does Nelson want to find out more about the Red-Headed League?

_____

_____

_____

NONLITERAL LANGUAGE What does Nelson mean when he says there was a "sea of red hair"?

_____

_____

_____

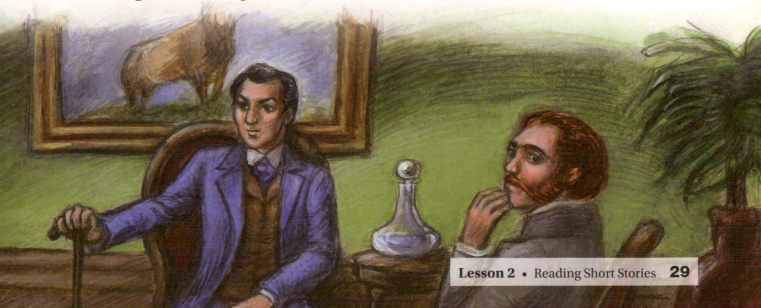

SEQUENCE Does Nelson hire the clerk before or after going to work for the Red-Headed League?

"This went on for eight weeks," Nelson told us. "Then, yesterday when I went to work, the office was locked. A sign on the door said 'The Red-Headed League is closed.' I was confused. I asked the landlord about the Red-Headed League. He said that he had never heard of it."

"Goodness, that's odd," I said.

"Well, it doesn't sound like there's been any crime," said Holmes. "You haven't been harmed. But it is quite unusual."

"You said that your clerk was new?" asked Holmes.

15   "Yes," said Nelson. "I hired him three months ago. He asked for very little pay. Maybe he spends too much time downstairs. He's been cleaning the cellar for weeks. Still, I can't complain. I know he could find a better job. I guess that's all I know to tell you."

"Thank you, Mr. Nelson. We'll look into it," Holmes said. I knew Holmes couldn't be stopped now. I've never met anyone as curious as Sherlock Holmes.

Holmes and I went out. We passed by Nelson's store. Holmes paused. He began naming everything he saw. "There's the market, then Nelson's shop. Right next door is the bank, then a coffee shop and the post office." I had seen Holmes do this before. He tried to notice every detail.

Holmes went into the bookshop. He came back out only a minute later. In the window, I saw the clerk. I asked Holmes if we had come just to look at Nelson's clerk.

"Not only him."

20 "What then?"

"The knees on his pants."

"And what did you see?" I asked.

Holmes didn't answer. He said he had some work to do. He asked me to join him that night.

"Be ready," said Holmes. "It may be dangerous."

CHARACTER TRAITS
Why does Holmes start naming the buildings near the bookstore?

_____

_____

_____

CHAPTERS Reread what Holmes says at the end of this page. Why do you think this is a good place to end the chapter?

_____

_____

_____

MAKING INFERENCES
After going through alleys, down steps, and through passageways, Holmes, Watson, Inspector Jones, and Mr. Cooper enter a large room. What inference can you make about what this room is? Underline the clues that led you to your inference.

_____

_____

ILLUSTRATIONS What does the picture on this page show about where this part of the story takes place? What mood does this picture create?

Chapter 3

_____

_____

_____

25   I arrived at Baker Street at 10:00. Holmes was talking to the local policeman, Inspector Jones. There was another man I didn't know.

"Watson," said Holmes, "this is Mr. Cooper. Cooper runs the bank next to Nelson's bookshop. But enough talk. Our time is short. I believe I know who is behind this Red-Headed League. Tonight we just might prevent a <mark>burglary</mark> of Cooper's bank."

We left, and soon we were near Nelson's bookstore. We hurried through dark alleys. Cooper opened a gate for us. He led us down many stairs and through passageways. At last we entered a large room. Holmes asked us to be completely silent. We turned out our lanterns and waited in the dark.

Nothing happened for an hour. Suddenly, a stream of light came from a hole in the floor. Then a hand came through the hole. The hand removed bricks from the floor. The hole grew bigger. Then, out of the hole climbed Nelson's clerk. A man with red hair followed.

"Stop, both of you!" shouted Inspector Jones. "You are under <mark>arrest</mark>!"

30 The men stopped. The inspector put them in handcuffs and led them away.

"Thank you, Holmes! Thank you, Watson!" said Cooper. "You stopped the burglars! How can I repay you?"

"I've been after that criminal John Clay for years," said Holmes. "To finally catch him is my reward."

Back at Baker Street, I begged Holmes to explain. How did he know that there would be a burglary that night?

"It's quite simple," he began. "I knew that this Red-Headed League was phony. Someone just wanted to get Nelson away from his shop every day. They made the notice for him alone. But why? The shop wasn't doing well. There wasn't much there to steal."

35 "True," I said.

"This new clerk was willing to work for very little money. That was strange. And the clerk spent a lot of time in the cellar. Why?"

Holmes went on, "When we visited Nelson's shop, I noticed the bank next door. And there in the bookstore was John Clay. I would know him anywhere. The knees on his pants were badly frayed. He must have been kneeling for a long time. It was then I was sure of it. Clay was digging a tunnel into the bank. And that other burglar we caught with him had red hair. His red hair must have given Clay the idea for the league."

DIALOGUE How does Mr. Cooper feel after the thieves are caught? How can you tell, based on what he says?

_____

_____

_____

COMPARE SETTINGS In "The Adventure of the Three Students," there are four settings. Three are in the same college building, and the other is at an inn. In "The Adventure of the Red-Headed League," how many settings are there? Name them.

_____

_____

_____

COMPARE STORY PLOTS Both this story and "The Adventure of the Three Students" are mystery stories. How do the turning points and resolutions of these stories differ?

_____

_____

_____

COMPARE THEMES A theme is a message or truth about life. One theme of "The Adventure of the Three Students" could be "Cheaters never win." Another theme could be "Sometimes life gives you a second chance." What is the theme of this story? How is it different from or similar to the themes of the first story?

_____

_____

_____

ASK AND ANSWER QUESTIONS Recall the question you asked at the beginning of the story. Have you found the answer? If you have, write it here.

_____

_____

_____

"But how did you know the burglary would be tonight?" I asked.

"It's Saturday, Watson. The bank is closed tomorrow. No one would know about the burglary until Monday. This would give the thieves time to get away."

"Simply amazing, Holmes," I said.

"Elementary, my dear Watson," said Sherlock Holmes.

Anchor Standard Discussion Questions

Discuss the following questions with your peer group. Then record your answers in the space provided.

1. What is Dr. Watson's opinion of his friend Sherlock Holmes? Does your own opinion of Holmes match Watson's? Explain why or why not. Support your answers with details from the text.

_____

_____

_____

_____

_____

2. Which mystery do you think was easier for Sherlock Holmes to solve, "The Adventure of the Red-Headed League" or "The Adventure of the Three Students"? Support your answer with details from the texts.

_____

_____

_____

_____

_____

Comprehension Check

1. Holmes tells Mr. Nelson that no crime has been committed against him. Why does Nelson want Holmes to solve the mystery?

_____

_____

_____

2. The Red-Headed League did not really inherit anyone's fortune. Why was it willing to pay Mr. Nelson so much money for so little work?

_____

_____

_____

3. Who is better at solving mysteries—Dr. Watson or Sherlock Holmes? How do you know?

_____

_____

_____

Read On Your Own

Read another story, "The Case of the Stolen Letter," independently. Apply what you learned in this lesson and check your understanding.

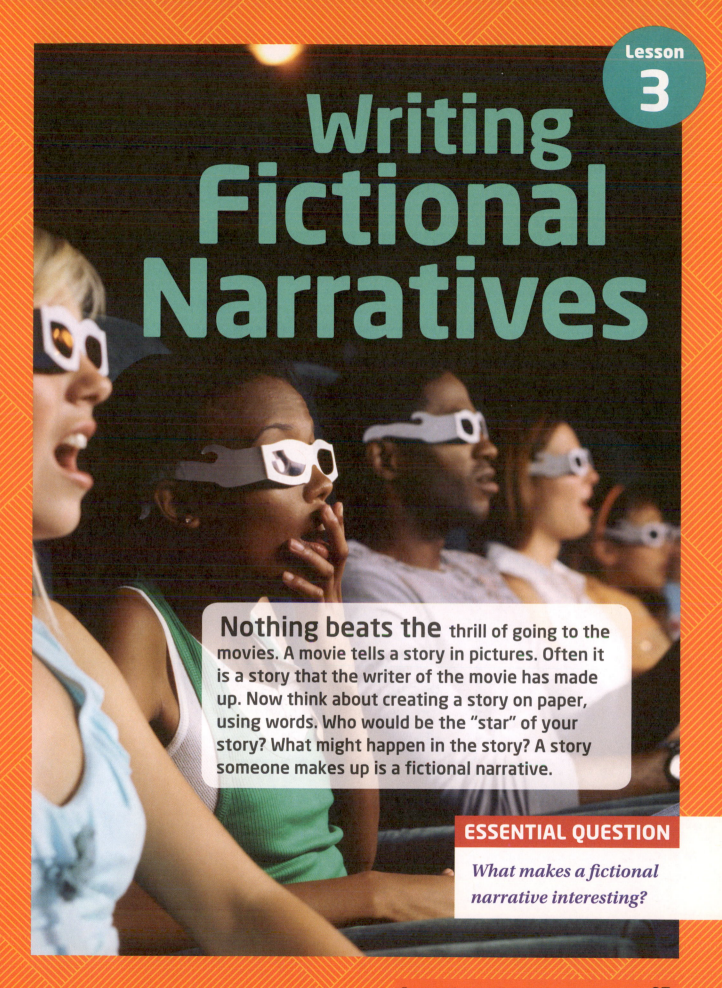

Writing Fictional Narratives

Nothing beats the thrill of going to the movies. A movie tells a story in pictures. Often it is a story that the writer of the movie has made up. Now think about creating a story on paper, using words. Who would be the "star" of your story? What might happen in the story? A story someone makes up is a fictional narrative.

ESSENTIAL QUESTION

What makes a fictional narrative interesting?

What's a Fictional Narrative?

Think of your favorite story. Is it a story about people, animals, or other creatures? Could the events of the story happen in real life, or do they happen in an imaginary place? Any one of these possible kinds of stories could be a fictional narrative.

In a **fictional narrative**, you tell a story that you make up. Read the ways to make your fictional narrative interesting.

Beginning
Introduce the characters and the situation.

Middle
Tell the events of your fictional narrative in order. Use dialogue to make your story exciting and realistic. Use description so the reader can picture what happens. Include a conflict, or problem, that the main character must solve.

Ending
A good ending is satisfying because it resolves the problem and tells how everything turns out.

Let's look at a fictional narrative.

Analyze a Mentor Text

This is an example of a fictional narrative by a third grader. Read it and then complete the activities in the boxes as a class.

A Change of Heart

Lucas was so excited, he could hardly finish tying his shoes. His big sister, Marie, was taking him to the county fair. There would be fun rides, popcorn, and cotton candy. There would be sheep, geese, and chickens. He couldn't wait to go. He ran out of his room. Then he stopped. He could hear Marie downstairs talking to her friends Holly and Geeta.

"Come on, Marie," said Geeta. "Leave him behind."

"We don't want an eight-year-old tagging along, do we?" added Holly.

"Not really, but I promised him earlier that I would take him," Marie said.

"Just take him another day. The fair will be here for a month," said Holly.

"I guess you're right," Marie said.

BEGINNING The writer gets the reader's attention by telling how Lucas feels. He also introduces the main characters and the situation to the reader. Draw a circle around the name of each of the main characters.

MIDDLE The writer uses dialogue to make the narrative convincing and realistic. Underline the dialogue on this page.

MIDDLE The writer uses description to bring the narrative to life. Put a star next to paragraphs with description.

ENDING The writer finishes with a good ending that satisfies the reader and tells how the story turns out. Circle the lines that make a good ending for this narrative.

Lucas felt crushed. His sister planned to leave him behind. He would miss the rides and the geese, sheep, and chickens. He stood there for a few seconds, and then, with his head hanging down, he went back to his room. He flopped on the bed, hiding his face in the pillows. A minute later, his sister walked in and sat next to him.

"You better go without me," said Lucas. "I don't feel so good."

Marie peered at Lucas. Looking so closely, she could see the hurt in his eyes. She suddenly realized he had heard everything. She gently stroked his hair. "I'm sorry, Lucas. I really do have fun with you. Please forgive me. I'd love to take you to the fair. My friends can come along, too."

Lucas sat up, all at once excited again. "Really?"

"Really." Marie gave him a big bear hug. "Which ride do you want to go on first?"

Think About It ▶ What part of the narrative do you like best?

Do you find the narrative interesting? Why or why not?

Vocabulary Study: Context Clues

The **context** of a word is all the other words around it. When you read, you may come to a word you don't know. Reading the words just before and just after the unfamiliar word can help you figure out its meaning. Context clues are words that will help you build your vocabulary.

For example, read the sentence below.

> Susan felt disappointed when she was not chosen to be in the school play.

Use context clues to define the word *disappointed*. Then check the word's meaning in a dictionary.

Look back at the fictional narrative "A Change of Heart" on pages 39–40. Find the words listed in the chart below. Look in the story for context clues for each word, and complete the chart. Use a dictionary to check the meaning. Then, for each word, write your own sentence using the word, or draw a picture that shows the word's meaning.

Word	crushed	peered
Meaning		
Context Clues		
Sentence or Picture		

Writing Process

You have read and looked at a fictional narrative. Now you are going to create your own by following these steps of the writing process.

1. Get Ready: Brainstorm Do you want to write about things that could really happen, or do you want to create a fantasy world? List some locations where your story could take place. Pick the one you like best.

2. Organize Use a graphic organizer to plan the beginning, middle, and ending and to organize your fictional narrative.

3. Draft Create the first draft of your fictional narrative. Don't worry too much about making mistakes. Get your ideas down.

4. Peer Review Work with a partner to evaluate and improve your draft.

5. Revise Use suggestions from your peer review to revise your work.

6. Edit Check your work carefully for spelling, punctuation, and grammar errors.

7. Publish Create a final version of your fictional narrative.

Writing Assignment

In this lesson, you will write your own fictional narrative. As you do, remember the elements of the mentor text that were most interesting. Read the following assignment.

> Write a story about a disagreement between a brother and a sister. Explain what the disagreement is about and what caused it. Tell how the disagreement is resolved with a good ending that satisfies the reader and tells how the story turns out. Your story should be three to five paragraphs long.

1. Get Ready: Brainstorm

The first step in writing a fictional narrative is to choose your characters and situation. Answer questions such as: Who are the main characters? What are they like? What are the characters doing or about to do?

Here's how the author of the mentor text brainstormed characters and situation.

Characters	Situation
Who are they? Lucas and Marie, brother and sister **What are they like?** Lucas is a normal eight-year-old boy. Marie is a caring big sister.	**What are the characters doing or about to do?** getting ready to go to a county fair

Try It!   Use a Brainstorming Graphic Organizer

Now use the chart below to help brainstorm the characters and situation for your own fictional narrative.

Characters	Situation
Who are they? _____ _____ **What are they like?** _____ _____	**What are the characters doing or about to do?** _____ _____

Brainstorm Details of Your Characters

It is important to think about what your characters are like. You can use a graphic organizer to help describe each character in more detail. Here is how the author of the mentor text used the graphic organizer.

CHARACTERS
The more things you know about the characters, the more interesting you can make them for the reader.

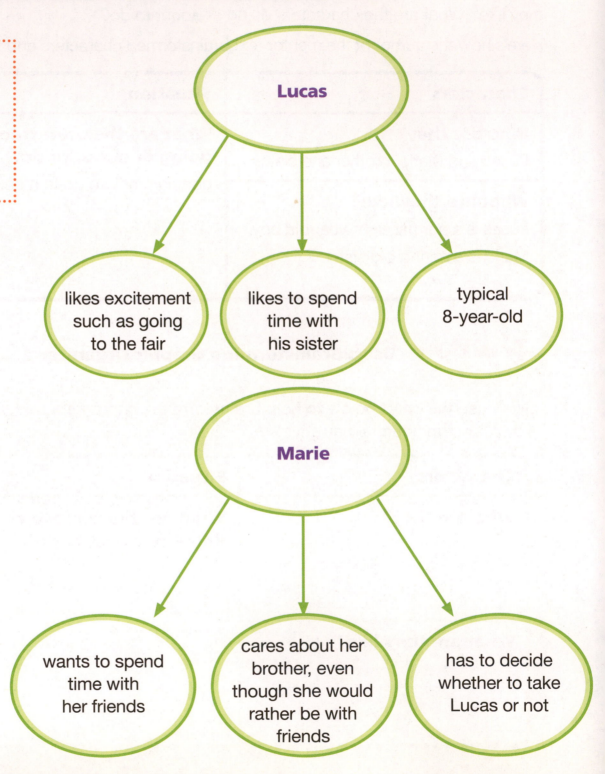

Try It!

Use a Graphic Organizer for Brainstorming

Now use the graphic organizer below to brainstorm the characters for your own fictional narrative. Draw more circles if you need them.

2. Organize

You are almost ready to begin a draft of your fictional narrative. You can use a sequence chart to put your characters into a situation and decide what happens to them. You can then refer to the sequence chart as you work through your draft. The writer of the mentor text completed this sequence chart.

BEGINNING Begin by introducing the characters and the situation.

> Lucas prepares to go to the county fair.

> Lucas overhears Marie talking to her friends. They don't want her to take Lucas to the fair.

> Lucas feels terrible and returns to his room.

MIDDLE Tell the events of the narrative in order. Plan dialogue and description to help you tell the events.

> Marie comes to Lucas's room. Lucas tells her to go to the fair without him.

> Marie sees that she has hurt Lucas. She apologizes and says she would like to take him to the fair.

ENDING Think of an ending that satisfies the reader and tells how everything turns out.

> Marie hugs Lucas, and they plan to go to the fair together.

Try It!

Organize Your Fictional Narrative

Now use the sequence chart below to organize the events of the narrative for your draft.

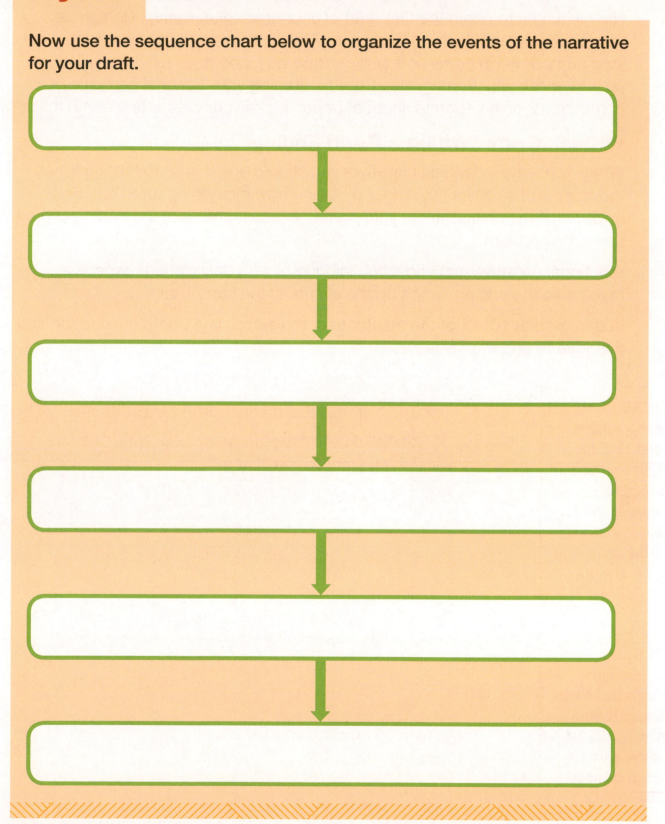

3. Draft

Now it is time to begin the first draft of your fictional narrative. Remember, your draft does not have to be perfect! This is the time to use your notes, get your story down in some sort of organized way, and have fun. You will have time to revise your writing later. Start by drafting your fictional narrative on a computer or on a separate sheet of paper. Make your characters come to life!

Writer's Craft: Writing a Good Ending

When you write a fictional narrative, you should end it in a way that finishes the story and satisfies the reader by telling how everything turns out. For example, if the characters in your narrative face a problem, the ending should solve the problem.

A fictional narrative can end with dialogue or with description. Either way, make sure the ending wraps up the events of the story well.

In paragraphs 10–11 of the mentor text, the author uses both description and dialogue to end the narrative.

DESCRIPTION
Read paragraphs 10 and 11 of the mentor text. Circle the words of description. With a classmate, discuss how the description helps to create a good ending.

> Lucas sat up, all at once excited again. "Really?"
>
> "Really." Marie gave him a big bear hug. "Which ride do you want to go on first?"

DIALOGUE
Underline the dialogue in the two paragraphs. With a classmate, discuss how the dialogue helps to create a satisfying ending.

Try It!

Write Your First Draft

On a computer or a separate sheet of paper, continue the draft of your fictional narrative. Remember to use description to help the reader picture what happens. Use dialogue to make the narrative convincing and realistic. Use this drafting checklist to help you as you write.

✔ A good beginning gets your reader's attention. You can begin with description or with dialogue.

✔ Introduce the characters at the beginning of the narrative, and describe the situation.

✔ Tell events in order in the middle of your narrative.

✔ Write a good ending that will satisfy the reader.

✔ Use dialogue and description to make the narrative exciting and bring it to life.

Tips for Writing Your First Draft

- Write down key phrases and pieces of dialogue before you begin writing. Sometimes this is a great warm-up to get you started!

- Think about a difficult situation that you have been in. But remember, in your narrative, *anything* can happen!

- Sometimes students think of good writing ideas while performing chores. If you get stuck, try cleaning your room!

4. Peer Review

After you finish your draft, you can work with a partner to review each other's drafts. Here is a draft of the mentor text. Read it with your partner. Together, answer the questions in the boxes. Then we'll see how the writer's classmate evaluated the draft.

An Early Draft:

BEGINNING In the draft, the writer does not introduce Marie clearly. What revisions would make it clear who Marie is?

MIDDLE Paragraph 2 could be told using dialogue instead of description, to make the scene come to life. What dialogue would you add?

ENDING The conclusion does not show whether Lucas accepts Marie's apology. What revisions would make the ending more satisfying for the reader?

A Change of Heart

Lucas was so excited he could hardly finish tying his shoes. Marie was taking him to the county fair. There would be fun rides, popcorn, and cotton candy. There would be sheep, geese, and chickens. He couldn't wait to go. He ran out of his room. Then he stopped. He could hear Marie downstairs talking to her friends Holly and Geeta.

Geeta told Marie that she should leave Lucas behind. Holly agreed with Geeta. She suggested that Marie take Lucas to the fair another day. Marie sounded sad, but she agreed with her friends.

Lucas was crushed. His sister was leaving him behind.

"You better go without me," said Lucas. "I don't feel so good."

Marie peered at Lucas. She stroked his hair. "I'm sorry, Lucas. I really do have fun with you. Please forgive me. I'd love to take you to the fair. My friends can come along or stay behind."

An Example Peer Review Form

This peer review form gives an example of how a classmate evaluated the draft of the mentor text shown on the last page.

The narrative includes a strong beginning, middle, and ending. **The beginning introduces the characters and the situation.**	**You did a good job of** introducing Lucas at the beginning.
	You could improve your fictional narrative by making it clear who Marie is.
In the middle, the writer tells the events in order.	**You did a good job of** describing Lucas's reaction to the girls' conversation.
	You could improve your fictional narrative by telling what happens after Lucas hears the conversation and before he tells Marie to go to the fair without him.
The writer uses dialogue to make the narrative convincing and realistic. **The writer uses description to help the reader picture the events.**	**You did a good job of** using dialogue to show how Lucas and Marie talk to each other.
	You could improve your fictional narrative by telling why Marie changes her mind.
The writer makes the ending satisfying to the reader and tells how everything turns out.	**You did a good job of** telling how Marie is sorry for hurting Lucas.
	You could improve your fictional narrative by telling whether Lucas accepts Marie's apology, and whether they go to the fair after all.

Try It!   Peer Review with a Partner

Now you are going to work with a partner to review each other's fictional narrative drafts. You will use the peer review form below. If you need help, look back at the mentor text writer's peer review form for suggestions.

The narrative includes a strong beginning, middle, and ending. **The beginning introduces the characters and the situation.**	You did a good job of You could improve your fictional narrative by
In the middle, the writer tells the events in order.	You did a good job of You could improve your fictional narrative by
The writer uses dialogue to make the narrative convincing and realistic. **The writer uses description to help the reader picture the events.**	You did a good job of You could improve your fictional narrative by
The writer makes the ending satisfying to the reader and tells how everything turns out.	You did a good job of You could improve your fictional narrative by

Try It! Record Key Peer Review Comments

Now it's time for you and your partner to share your comments with each other. Listen to your partner's feedback, and write down the key comments in the left column. Then write some ideas for improving your draft in the right column.

My review says that my beginning	I will
My review says that my characters	I will
My review says that my situation	I will
My review says that the middle	I will
My review says that the ending	I will

Use the space below to write anything else you notice about your draft that you think you can improve.

5. Revise

In this step of the writing process, you work on parts of your draft that need improvement. Use the peer review form that your classmate completed to help you. Also use your own ideas about how to improve each part of your fictional narrative. This checklist includes some things to think about as you get ready to revise.

Revision Checklist

✓ Does my beginning introduce the characters and situation well? Is the problem presented clearly?

✓ Does the middle tell the events in order?

✓ Is the ending satisfying and does it tell how things turn out?

✓ Do I use dialogue to make the narrative convincing and realistic? Do I use description to help the reader picture events?

✓ Do I use words and phrases that signal time to show the event order?

LANGUAGE THAT SIGNALS TIME

Language that signals time tells the order of events. Underline words that signal time in this passage. What other words could the writer have used to signal time in the passage?

_____

_____

Writer's Craft: Using Words and Phrases That Signal Time to Show Event Order

Using words and phrases that signal time helps to show the order of events in your fictional narrative. For example, using *first* and *next* tells the reader what happened first and what happened after that. The phrases *after lunch* and *in a little while* also signal time to show the order of events. Now look at the mentor text for examples of language that signals time.

> Lucas felt crushed. His sister planned to leave him behind. He would miss the rides and the geese, sheep, and chickens. He stood there for a few seconds, and then, with his head hanging down, he went back to his room. He flopped on the bed, hiding his face in the pillows. A minute later, his sister walked in and sat next to him.

Try It!   Revise Your Fictional Narrative

Showing the order of events is an important part of revising. Practice using words that signal time in the following paragraph. Read each sentence. On the lines below the paragraph, write the words you would add to signal time.

I love getting ready for a family vacation. _____, I do research on the computer to find things to see. _____, I make a list of all the clothes I'll need. _____, I pack my backpack with books and other things I want to take along.

Second sentence: _____

Third sentence: _____

Fourth sentence: _____

Writing Assignment

Now it's time to revise the draft of your fictional narrative. Continue working on a computer or on a separate sheet of paper. Review the assignment, repeated below, and the checklist. Doing so will help you make sure that you have included everything you need.

Write a story about a disagreement between a brother and a sister. Explain what the disagreement is about and what caused it. Tell how the disagreement is resolved with a good ending that satisfies the reader and tells how the story turns out. Your story should be three to five paragraphs long.

6. Edit

After revising your fictional narrative, you will edit it. When you edit, you read very carefully to be sure to find any mistakes in your writing. Here's a checklist of some things to look for as you edit.

Editing Checklist

✓ Did you indent each paragraph?

✓ Are all of your sentences complete?

✓ Did you begin each sentence with a capital letter?

✓ Does each sentence end with the correct punctuation?

✓ Have you used commas correctly?

✓ Are all of your words spelled correctly?

You can use these editing marks to mark any errors you find.

^ Add	⊙ Period	↷ Add comma
≡ Change a lowercase letter to a capital letter		

This is a paragraph from the draft of the mentor text showing how to use editing marks.

> Lucas was so excited he could hardly finish tying his shoes. marie was taking him to the county fair. There would be fun rides popcorn and cotton candy. There would be sheep, geese, and chickens. He couldn't wait to go. He ran out of room then he stopped. He could hear Marie downstairs talking to her friends holly and Geeta.

Language Focus: Using Nouns and Verbs

A noun names a person, place, thing, or idea. To make a regular noun name more than one person, place, thing, or idea, add *-s, -es,* or change a *y* to *i* and add *-es.*

Examples: cat, cats   lady, ladies

An irregular noun takes a different form when it names more than one person, place, thing, or idea.

Examples: man, men   foot, feet

A verb is an action word. It tells what a subject does or is. With a regular verb, add *-s* or *-es* to tell what the subject is doing right now, and *-d* or *-ed* to tell what the subject did in the past.

Examples: he wants, he wanted   she pets, she petted
he wishes, he wished

An irregular verb takes a different form for the present than it does for the past.

Example: This year, I **am** eight. Last year, I **was** seven.

A subject and verb should agree when the subject noun names a single person or thing and also when it names more than one person or thing.

Examples:

  Jane rides her bike to the park every Saturday.

  Alex and Nina ride their bikes to school.

Lucas felt crushed. His sister planned to leave him behind. He would miss the rides and the geese, sheep, and chickens. He stood there for a few seconds, and then, with his head hanging down, he went back to his room. He flopped on the bed, hiding his face in the pillows. A minute later, his sister walked in and sat next to him.

NOUNS AND VERBS
Read these sentences from the mentor text. Underline six verbs. Put a star by six nouns that name more than one thing. Find the two of these nouns that are irregular, and draw a box around each.

Try It!   Language and Editing Practice

Complete each sentence with the correct form of the noun or verb.

1. Lucas wanted to see _____ at the fair. (geese, gooses)

2. "Yesterday I _____ a story about a silly goose," he said. (readed, read)

3. "The goose _____ she could lay golden eggs." (thinked, thought)

4. "That _____ certainly a silly goose," said Lucas's sister. (was, am, are)

5. "Maybe we should go see the _____ instead," said Lucas. (sheep, sheeps)

Now use editing marks to correct the errors in subject/verb agreement in this paragraph.

When Dashiell spends the day with his father, they has a good time. First, they swims in the lake together. Next, he catch as many fish as they can. Later, one of them sing a song, and the other joins in. They ends the day at the drive-in and eat a meal together.

Try It!   Edit Your Fictional Narrative

Now edit your fictional narrative. Use this checklist and the editing marks you have learned to correct any errors you find.

- [ ] Did you indent each paragraph?

- [ ] Are all of your sentences complete?

- [ ] Did you begin each sentence with a capital letter?

- [ ] Does each sentence end with the correct punctuation?

- [ ] Have you used commas correctly?

- [ ] Are all of your words spelled correctly?

- [ ] Have you used nouns and verbs properly? Do subjects and verbs agree?

Editing Tips

- Read your writing aloud. This will help you discover missing words and awkward phrases. Ask yourself, "Does that sound right?"

- Read your writing over at a slow pace at least two times. When you are looking at small details, one reading is not enough!

- Set aside your writing for a short period before editing. You may be able to find errors more easily.

7. Publish

On a computer or a separate sheet of paper, create a neat final draft of your fictional narrative. Correct all errors that you identified while editing your draft. Be sure to give your fictional narrative an interesting title.

The final step is to publish your fictional narrative. Here are some different ways you might choose to share your work.

- Create a class anthology that collects your and your classmates' fictional narratives.

- With a small group of your classmates, act out your fictional narrative on stage as a play.

- Record a dramatic reading of your fictional narrative on video.

- Illustrate your fictional narrative with pictures of characters and events.

Technology Suggestions

- Upload your fictional narrative onto your class or school blog.
- Scan illustrations for your fictional narrative, and create a printed booklet.

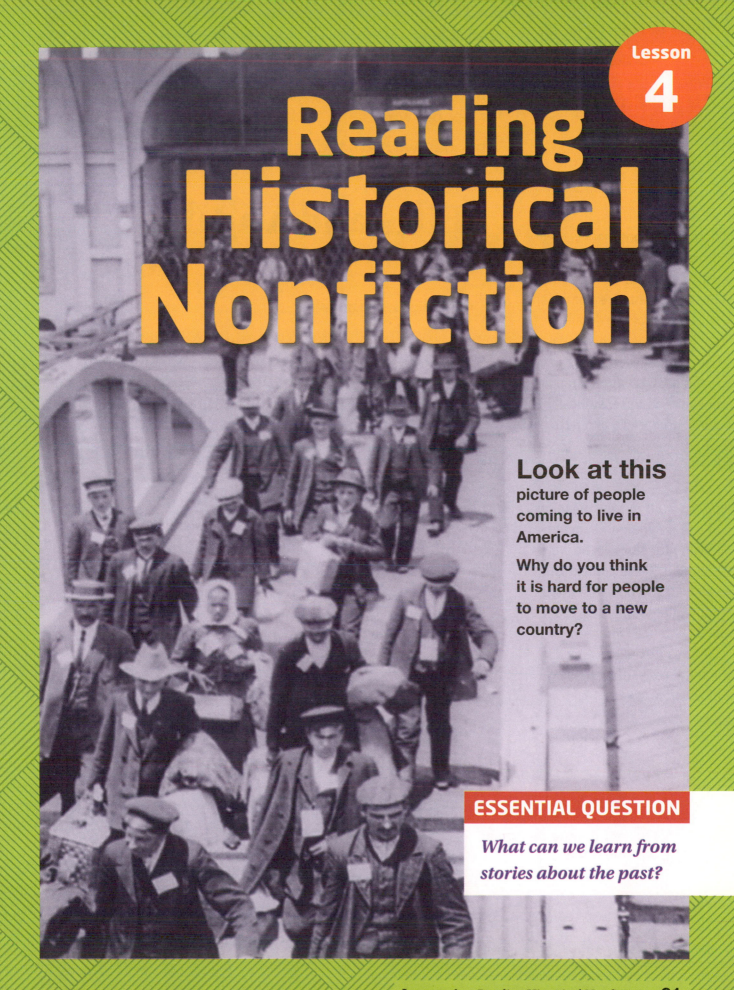

Reading Historical Nonfiction

Look at this picture of people coming to live in America.

Why do you think it is hard for people to move to a new country?

ESSENTIAL QUESTION

What can we learn from stories about the past?

Consider ▶ What were the first days in a new country like for people who came to the United States?

What can we learn today from challenges people faced in the past?

HISTORICAL NONFICTION Accounts about real events or people from the past are called historical nonfiction. These accounts are nonfiction because all of the details are true. They are historical because the events happened in the past. What real people or events is this historical nonfiction article about?

CONTEXT CLUES You can often figure out the meaning of a word you don't know by looking for clues in the words around it. These context clues can help you understand the unfamiliar word. Look at the first sentence in paragraph 1. What context clue can help you figure out the meaning of *immigrant*?

Ellis and Angel: Islands of Hope

Land of Immigrants

1   The United States is a country with many immigrants. Some families arrived recently from faraway places. Other families settled here long ago. In the late 1800s and early 1900s, millions of immigrants came to the United States. Many came to escape poverty and hunger. Others came to find freedom and opportunity.

    Before beginning new lives in the United States, newcomers had to pass through immigration stations. At these stations, officials asked the immigrants many questions and checked their health. Those who passed the inspection were allowed into the country. Ellis Island and Angel Island were two of the most important immigration stations. Ellis Island was off the coast of New York City. Angel Island was across the country, near San Francisco, California.

Soon after Ellis Island opened, thousands of immigrants arrived each day.

Arriving at Ellis Island

Back in the early 1900s, ships full of new immigrants arrived daily in New York Harbor. They came from Ireland, Germany, Italy, Poland, and other countries. Most rich passengers entered the United States easily. If these passengers could afford nice rooms on the ships, officers thought they would have money to survive in the United States. Poorer passengers were taken to Ellis Island. Sometimes Ellis Island was too crowded to fit more people. When this happened, new immigrants spent days waiting aboard their ships.

After entering Ellis Island, the newcomers had to answer many questions. Officials wanted to know where they came from. They asked where the immigrants were planning to live. What would they do for work? Could they read or write? Had they ever been in jail? Immigrants worried that a wrong answer would keep them from entering the United States.

Days on Ellis Island

5   Life at Ellis Island could be uncomfortable. The noise in the room where immigrants waited never ended. Dozens of languages blended together into a constant roar of noise. Immigrants sat on long wooden benches for hours. They stood in long lines with hundreds of others, waiting to speak with officials.

MAIN IDEA AND DETAILS
The most important point in a piece of writing is called the main idea. It is often stated at the beginning of a paragraph or article. Other facts or ideas that tell more about the main idea are supporting details. The main idea of this part of the article is: "Life at Ellis Island could be uncomfortable." What supporting details can you find that tell more about the main idea?

Doctors made sure immigrants were healthy before they left Ellis Island. Sick people would spread diseases and be unable to work.

ASK AND ANSWER QUESTIONS Asking questions and looking for the answers as you read can help you understand an article better. Look back at paragraphs 6 and 7. What questions do you have about how people lived on Ellis Island after reading these paragraphs? How might looking for the answers to these questions help you better understand the article?

Doctors at Ellis Island checked to make sure every immigrant was healthy. Some who were sick were sent to the island's hospital. They had to get better before they could enter the country.

Many immigrants spent only a few hours at Ellis Island. A few were held there for weeks. Immigrants ate in a dining room with hundreds of other people. People ate foods they had never seen before, such as bananas. They slept among strangers on bunk beds in crowded rooms. Families were separated, and men and women slept in different rooms.

Immigrants could change their money for American dollars at a bank on Ellis Island. They could send mail or telegrams. They could buy train tickets for the next part of their journey. Children could use the playground on the building's roof.

After a few days, most immigrants received a landing card. A landing card served as legal identification and as a record that the person could now enter the country. However, about one out of every fifty people was not allowed to enter. These people were sent back to their home countries.

10   Altogether, more than 12 million people came through Ellis Island from 1892 to 1954. This was their very first experience in America.

Ellis Island Today

The immigration center at Ellis Island was open until 1954. In 1965, Ellis Island became part of the Liberty National Monument. It would be protected for years to come. In 1990, the main building at Ellis Island opened as a museum. Visitors to the museum can watch films about the people who immigrated through Ellis Island. Exhibits show passports and suitcases that immigrants brought with them. About two million people visit this historic place each year. They come to learn about the brave people who came to the United States with nothing but the hope of a building a new life.

AUTHOR'S PURPOSE
Authors have different reasons for writing. Sometimes the author's reason, or purpose, is to share information or to inform the reader. At other times an author may want to make the reader laugh or to get the reader to agree with the author's opinion. What is the author's purpose in this article—to inform, to amuse, or to change an opinion?

Visitors have to take a ferry to visit the Ellis Island Immigration Museum.

Angel Island Immigration Center

In 1910, another U.S. immigration center opened. This one was on Angel Island in San Francisco Bay. Some people called it the "Ellis Island of the West."

Laws passed in the 1880s made it harder to enter the United States from China than from other countries. Many of the people arriving at Angel Island were Chinese immigrants. Most people were kept on the island for two to three weeks. Others stayed for months or even years. While at Angel Island, they had no way of communicating with family or friends outside of Angel Island. Many worried that they might never enter the United States.

Life at Angel Island

Conditions at Angel Island were more harsh than they were at Ellis Island. The newcomers lived in crowded rooms. They slept in metal bunks. They were usually given a watery rice porridge to eat. The grounds were surrounded by high metal fences topped with barbed wire. Days passed slowly. Immigrants played card games or mah-jongg, a game invented in China, to fill the hours.

Hundreds of thousands of immigrants, mostly from China, were processed at Angel Island.

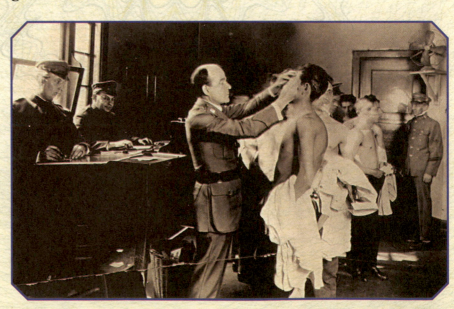

15   Like the immigrants at Ellis Island, those at Angel Island were asked many questions. This could be very confusing. The officials who spoke Chinese often spoke a different form of the language than the immigrants. The officials asked difficult questions. They wanted to determine if certain immigrants were actually related to U.S. citizens, as they claimed. The officials might ask questions about an immigrant's ancestors and home village. They might ask how many steps there were leading out of a family's back door. They might even ask where an immigrant sat in his or her village schoolhouse. They also spoke with witnesses for the immigrants, to check if their stories were true. This could take a long time, especially if the witnesses lived in other states.

The officials often did not trust the immigrants' stories. They wanted to make sure the immigrants' accounts matched those of their families. Simple mistakes sometimes meant that an immigrant would be sent back to his or her home country. Overall, about one out of four Chinese immigrants was not allowed into the United States.

COMPARE AND CONTRAST
Immigrants at Ellis Island were asked questions about what they would do for work and if they could read or write. How are the questions that officials asked immigrants at Angel Island different? How are they similar?

Angel Island Today

From 1910 to 1940, more than 250,000 immigrants passed through Angel Island. Today, the island is a state park. There is a museum in the old immigration station. Visitors come to read poems that immigrants wrote on the walls. They come to learn the stories of America's Asian immigrants.

After being abandoned for many years, the buildings on Angel Island were restored starting in 1976. Angel Island State Park has become a tourist destination.

Comprehension Check

Look back at "Ellis and Angel: Islands of Hope." How was Ellis Island different from Angel Island? How was it the same? Use the Venn diagram below to list your ideas. In the center, write what the two locations had in common. On the sides, list details that are different between the two immigration stations.

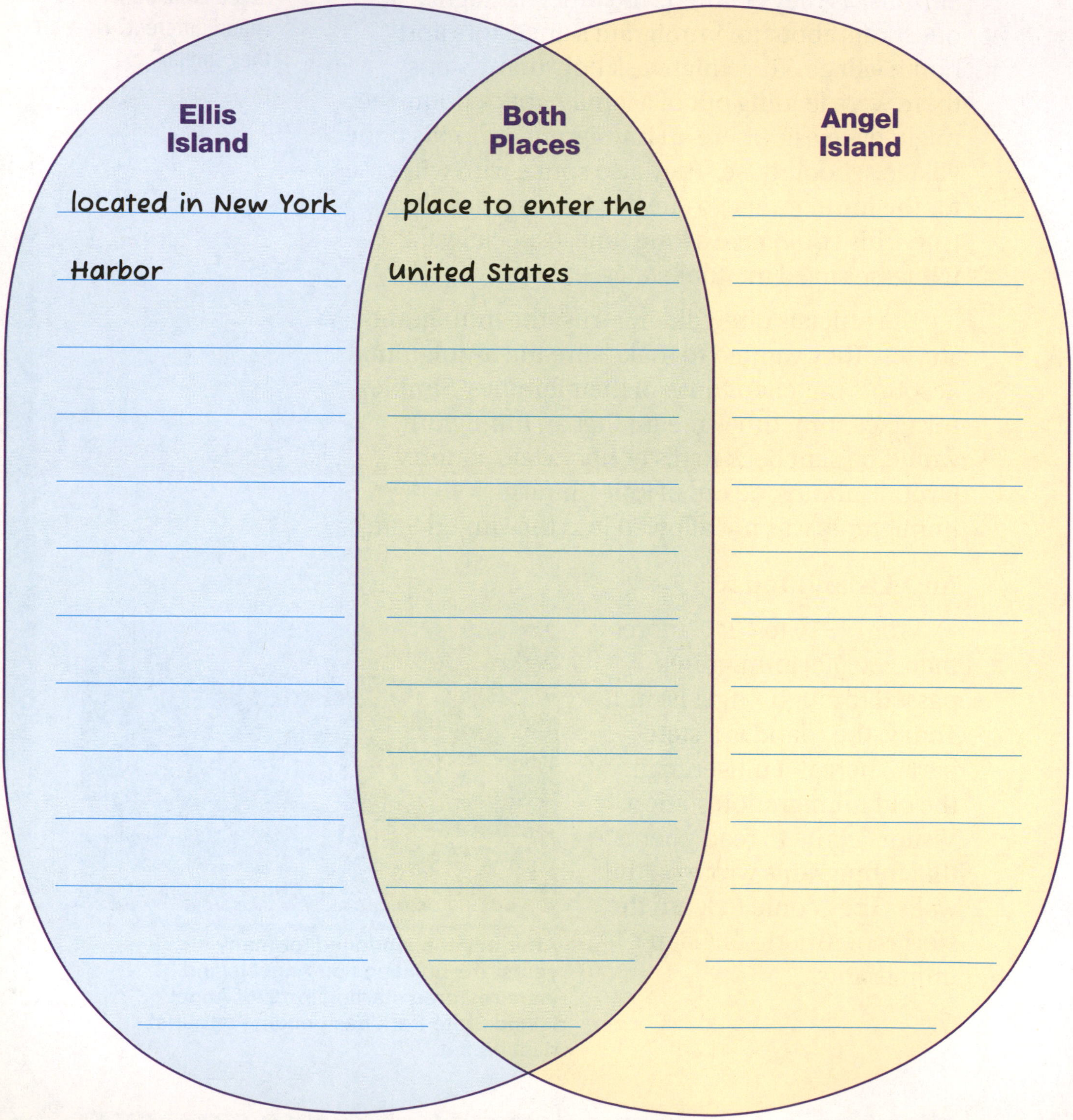

Ellis Island

located in New York

Harbor

Both Places

place to enter the

United States

Angel Island

Vocabulary

Use the word map below to help you define and use one of the highlighted vocabulary words from the Share and Learn reading or another word your teacher assigns you.

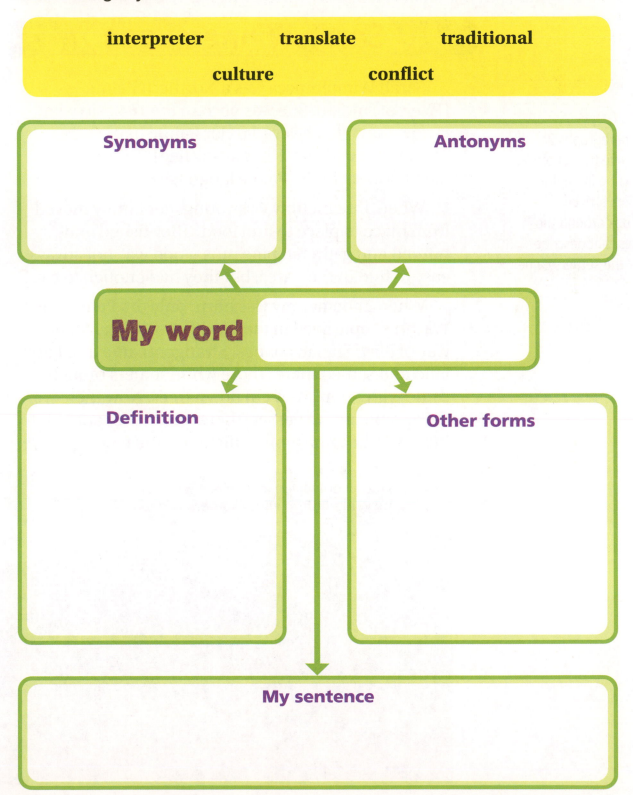

interpreter   translate   traditional

culture   conflict

Synonyms

Antonyms

My word

Definition

Other forms

My sentence

Consider ▶ What challenges did Native Americans face when other people came to America?

How did Native Americans respond to those challenges?

Sarah Winnemucca

1 Sarah Winnemucca was a Northern Paiute (PY-yoot) Indian. She was born in the 1840s in what is now the state of Nevada. Her Paiute name was Thocmetony (THOCK-muh-toe-nee). This means "shell flower" in the Paiute language.

When Thocmetony was young, her family moved from place to place to find food. They fished and hunted and gathered pine nuts. Food was not always easy to find in their area, but they had enough to eat.

When Thocmetony was born, only the Paiute and Washo people lived in the area. But soon the Paiute way of life began to change. Strangers came into Paiute land and settled there. These white settlers brought cattle with them. They cut down trees. Now there were fewer pine nuts to gather. There were fewer animals to hunt. Life became more difficult for the Paiute people.

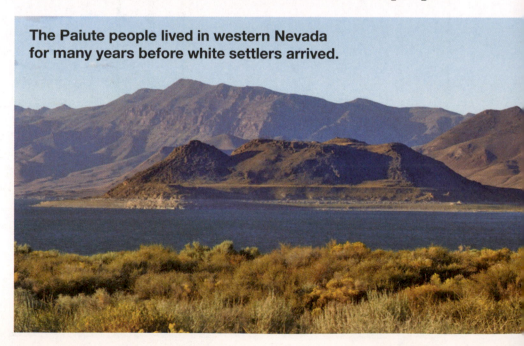

The Paiute people lived in western Nevada for many years before white settlers arrived.

Many Paiutes wanted to fight. They wanted to drive the strangers out of their land. Thocmetony's grandfather, Truckee (TRUHK-ee), had a different idea. He believed that these strangers were brothers to the Paiutes. He believed that the only way the Paiutes could survive was to learn to live with the white settlers.

5   Thocmetony was afraid of the white strangers. In 1850, when she was six, Truckee decided to take her to California. He wanted her to meet these people and see how they lived. In California, she met many good people. She learned to be less afraid of them.

Truckee wanted his grandchildren to learn the ways of other people. Thocmetony began to learn English. She was given the name Sarah.

When Sarah was thirteen, she and her sister, Elma, went to live with a white family in Utah. They learned to speak and write in English. Sarah was a quick learner. She had a special gift for language. By the time she was fourteen, Sarah could speak five different languages.

COMPARE AND CONTRAST Find the paragraph that describes how Truckee's ideas about the strangers were different from the ideas of other Paiutes. Underline a sentence that tells about Truckee's ideas. Circle a sentence that tells about other Paiutes' ideas.

ASK AND ANSWER QUESTIONS What information does the author provide to show that Sarah was a quick learner?

_____

_____

_____

AUTHOR'S PURPOSE What do you think was the author's purpose for writing this article? What details gave you that idea?

_____

_____

_____

Sarah Winnemucca worked all of her life to help the Paiute people.

MAIN IDEA AND DETAILS The author writes that life for the Paiutes grew worse. Underline the sentence that tells this. Then circle two details that support this idea.

Meanwhile, life for the Paiutes became worse. More and more strangers came. They took away Paiute land and food. Sometimes they killed Paiute people for no reason.

Sarah knew she needed to do something. She began to fight for her people with the only tool she had. She began to use her skill with words.

10   At the time, people in the United States knew that there were problems between Native Americans and white settlers. Most people had heard only the settlers' side of the story. Sarah Winnemucca wanted them to learn the Native Americans' side, too.

Sarah Winnemucca worked as an ==interpreter==. She helped people who spoke different languages understand one another. She would ==translate== messages in English into the Paiute language. She explained Paiute beliefs to the white settlers. Sarah Winnemucca began giving speeches about the Paiute people. She wanted others to understand their way of life.

In 1880, Sarah Winnemucca went to Washington, D.C. She gave many speeches there about the Paiute people. She discovered that crowds of people listened to her when she wore her ==traditional== Paiute clothes. They would come to the theater to hear her share stories about the Paiutes. She met with the president of the United States and other powerful people. She wanted these people to help protect Paiute lands.

Sarah Winnemucca wrote a book about her people and their ways. It was called *Life Among the Piutes: Their Wrongs and Claims*. She described how the settlers had affected Paiute life. It was the first book written by a Native American woman.

Sarah Winnemucca opened a school in Nevada. She taught students in both English and the Paiute language. She kept working to help different people understand each other. Sarah Winnemucca did many things to help her people.

This statue of Sarah Winnemucca now stands inside the U.S. Capitol in Washington, D.C.

CONTEXT CLUES
Which words in paragraph 11 help you understand the meaning of ==translate==? Draw a box around each word.

MAIN IDEA AND DETAILS Recall the details about Sarah Winnemucca that you have read. What do you think is the main idea of this article?

_____

_____

_____

Consider ▶ What new things do you learn about Sarah Winnemucca in this article?

Why is it valuable to read different articles about the same subject?

A Great Woman

1   Sarah Winnemucca is one of the most important Native American women in American history. She did a lot of things in her life to help Native Americans. She was an interpreter, a teacher, and a writer. She worked hard to help people from different cultures understand each other.

Winnemucca the Interpreter

Winnemucca lived at a time when life was often difficult for Native Americans. She was a member of the Paiute Nation. Settlers were moving west across America and were sometimes taking the Paiutes' land. Conflict was common. Many Native Americans did not have contact with settlers except through fighting.

TEXT FEATURES Before reading the text on this page, look at the title and headings. What is one thing you think Sarah Winnemucca did that was great? Underline the words that are clues.

_____

_____

_____

CONTEXT CLUES Find a word in paragraph 2 that helps you understand the meaning of conflict. Circle the word.

Winnemucca was different. Unlike many Paiute people, she spent a lot of time with people of other cultures when she was young. She moved to California with her grandfather when she was six years old. There she learned to speak Spanish and English. Then, when she was thirteen years old, Winnemucca moved to Utah. There she learned to read and write. Her English became excellent.

Winnemucca's language skills were important when war broke out between the Paiutes and the settlers. She became an interpreter. Winnemucca used her special skills to help Native Americans and settlers understand each other.

Winnemucca the Teacher

5   Winnemucca was also a teacher. She spoke out about Paiute life. She gave speeches in California. She told people about the difficult conditions her people were facing. Many were killed in war, and many were sick. She talked to officials about protecting Paiute lands.

In 1880, Winnemucca traveled to Washington, D.C. She gave hundreds of speeches in Washington and in other cities. In Washington, Winnemucca spoke to Congress about the Paiute people. She even spoke with President Rutherford B. Hayes.

Winnemucca also started a school for Native American children. Students at the school learned about the Native American way of life. They also learned to read and write. Winnemucca believed these skills were important for Native Americans to learn.

LOGICAL CONNECTIONS What words signal that the author is contrasting Sarah Winnemucca with other Native Americans? How does the author say Winnemucca was unlike other Native Americans?

_____

_____

_____

COMPARE AND CONTRAST Look at the section "Winnemucca the Writer." Underline details about Winnemucca's book that are the same as the details you read in the first article. Circle details about her book that are different.

_____

_____

_____

MAIN IDEA AND DETAILS The main idea of the last paragraph is "Winnemucca's book was the most important thing she did for the Paiute people." What details support this claim?

_____

_____

_____

AUTHOR'S PURPOSE How do the titles and headings help readers understand the author's purpose for writing this article?

_____

_____

_____

Winnemucca the Writer

In 1883, Winnemucca became the first Native American woman to publish a book in English. In her book, she told the history of the Paiute Nation and described how they lived. She also told the story of her life and shared letters she received.

Winnemucca's book was the most important thing she did for the Paiute people. It was the first book to describe the Paiute way of life. People everywhere could learn about the Paiutes, not only people who listened to Winnemucca speak. Even today, people read her book to learn about Native American life in the past. Winnemucca's book will keep her story alive for many years to come.

Anchor Standard Discussion Question

Discuss the following question with your peer group. Then record your answer in the space provided.

1. Which of the two articles about Sarah Winnemucca do you think would be better to include in a history book? Why? Support your answer with details from both texts.

_____

_____

_____

_____

_____

_____

_____

_____

_____

_____

_____

_____

Comprehension Check

1. How are Sarah Winnemucca and the Paiute people similar to the immigrants you read about in "Ellis and Angel: Islands of Hope"?

_____

_____

_____

2. What topic was the main subject of Sarah Winnemucca's book?

_____

_____

_____

3. Why do you think the author of "A Great Woman" did not include details about where or when Sarah Winnemucca was born?

_____

_____

_____

Read On Your Own

Read another historical nonfiction text, "Harriet Tubman," independently. Apply what you learned in this lesson and check your understanding.

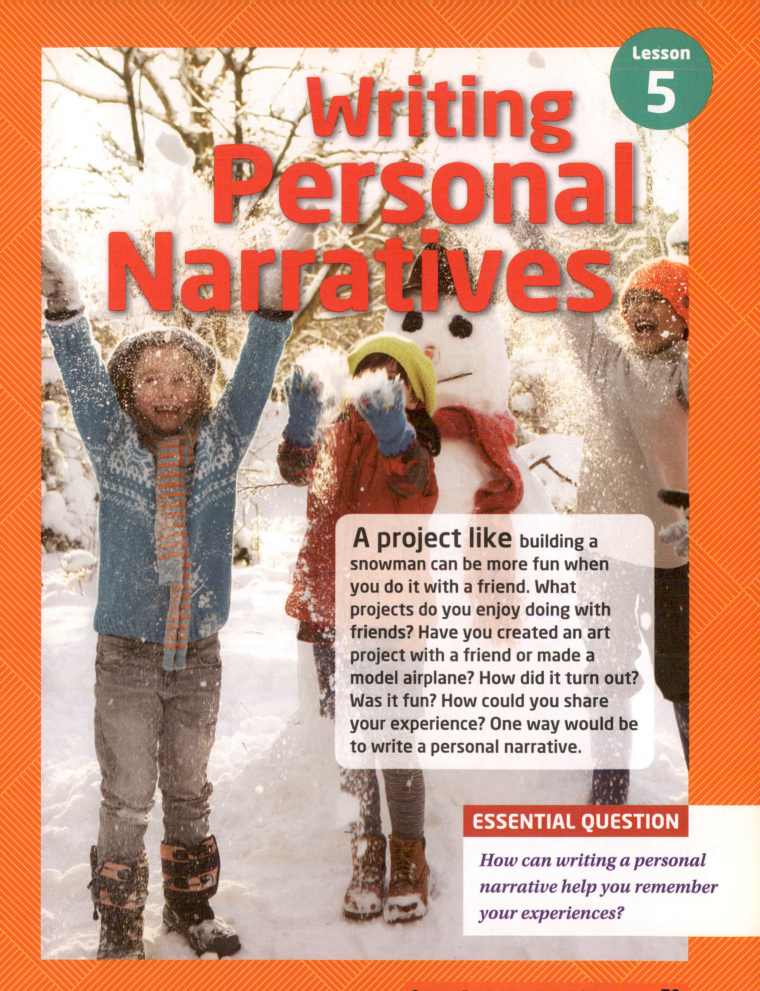

Writing Personal Narratives

A project like building a snowman can be more fun when you do it with a friend. What projects do you enjoy doing with friends? Have you created an art project with a friend or made a model airplane? How did it turn out? Was it fun? How could you share your experience? One way would be to write a personal narrative.

ESSENTIAL QUESTION

How can writing a personal narrative help you remember your experiences?

What's a Personal Narrative?

Perhaps you need help with a science or art project. Or you want to make a model or build a birdhouse. These are good activities to do with a friend. They could all turn into personal narratives. You can write about any experience in a personal narrative.

In a **personal narrative**, you describe an event or series of events that happened to you. You share what was funny or what you liked about the experience. Here are some ways to make your personal narrative interesting.

Beginning
Tell about yourself and the project. Give a hint at what lies ahead.

Middle
Describe the important events in the order they took place. Include dialogue to show the characters' words, thoughts, and feelings, and exact details that give a clear picture of what happened.

Ending
Tell how the project turned out and how you felt about it.

Let's look at a personal narrative.

Analyze a Mentor Text

This is an example of an effective personal narrative by a third grader. Read it and then complete the activities in the boxes as a class.

The Day We Built a Snow Penguin

Last year, something happened that I will always remember. In January, it snowed almost two feet! School was closed, so I built a giant snowman with my best friend, Linda. Well, it wasn't actually a snowman. It was a snow penguin.

We worked all morning on our creation. When we got cold, we went inside to warm up. My mom gave us hot chocolate and then we headed back outside to continue building. After a couple of hours, we had gotten halfway up the penguin's body. The penguin was taller than we were. It was impossible to finish it!

"How are we going to make its head?" asked Linda.

"I don't know," I told her. "We'll never reach to the top."

"I have an idea!" she said. "Let's push him over and make him lie down. He could look as if he's swimming on his back. That way we will be able to reach all parts of him."

"Great idea!" I said. "Let's do it."

BEGINNING The beginning tells what the project was and when it happened. The writer uses lively details. Circle a detail that got your attention.

MIDDLE The writer organizes events in a clear time order. Underline a word or phrase that shows when something happened.

SENSORY DETAILS
The writer uses sensory details to help the reader feel and see what happened. Underline two of these details in the narrative.

ENDING How does the writer feel about the project at the end? Draw a star next to the part that tells you how the writer feels.

We stood in front of the snow penguin, counted to three, and then pushed him over. What a mistake! Instead of lying on its back, the penguin fell into a hundred pieces.

"Oh no!" I yelled. "He's broken!" We stared at the broken penguin for several minutes. All our hard work was undone.

"Don't worry," said Linda. "We can rebuild."

I felt glad that Linda still wanted to work on the penguin with me. But my mittens were wet, and my feet felt like icicles. I didn't want to start all over again.

Then Linda said, "I know. Let's have another cup of hot chocolate first."

What a great idea! The hot chocolate was like an electric blanket for my insides. After that, I thought about what a fun day this had been. We went back out and fixed our penguin, and he looked amazing!

Think About It ▶ Why do you think the writer wanted to tell about this experience?

How does the writer help you to feel and see what happened?

Vocabulary Study: Prefixes and Root Words

A **root word** is a base word with no prefix or suffix. It contains the word's core meaning. A **prefix** comes at the beginning of a word. The prefix changes the meaning of the word. Work with your class or a partner to fill the blank boxes with a word that includes the prefix.

Prefix	Meaning	Root Word with Prefix
pre-	before	precook
im–	not	
re-	again	
un–	not	

Look back at the personal narrative about the snow penguin. Find two words with prefixes, and complete the chart below. Use a dictionary to check each word's meaning. Then write your own sentence using the word.

Word
Prefix
Meaning
Sentence

Word
Prefix
Meaning
Sentence

Writing Process

Now that you have looked at an example of a personal narrative, you are going to create your own by following the steps below.

1. Get Ready: Brainstorm List several projects you might want to write about. Choose projects you enjoyed doing with friends. Think of what you remember best about the projects.

2. Organize Use a graphic organizer to organize events and details.

3. Draft Create the first draft of your personal narrative.

4. Peer Review Work with a partner to improve your draft.

5. Revise Use suggestions from your peer review to revise your work.

6. Edit Check your work carefully for spelling, punctuation, and grammar errors.

7. Publish Create a final version of your personal narrative.

Writing Assignment

In this lesson, you will write your own personal narrative. As you create this narrative, remember the parts of the mentor text that worked best. Read the following assignment.

> Think of a project that you worked on with a friend. Choose something you enjoyed. Why was the project important to you? Was it helpful to work with a friend? How did the project turn out? Did anything funny happen? What did you learn? What would you like to share about the experience with an audience?
>
> Write three to five paragraphs describing the project you and your friend worked on. Get your readers interested in your experience!

1. Get Ready: Brainstorm a Topic

The first step in writing a personal narrative is to choose your topic. Begin by listing several projects you have worked on with friends. For each one, write what was fun or how it turned out.

Here's how the author of the mentor narrative captured some memories.

concert poster	snow penguin	tree house
Annie and I made a big poster for the band concert. It was great!	Our snow penguin broke into pieces, but Linda and I had fun working on it.	The project was too hard, so we never finished the tree house.

Try It! Use a Graphic Organizer

Now use the chart below to help capture memories for your own personal narrative. Choose projects that you enjoyed doing with a friend.

Brainstorm Ideas for Your Topic

You can use a graphic organizer to help capture ideas and details for your personal narrative. Here is how the author of the mentor text used the graphic organizer.

BEGINNING Tell what the project is, when you did it, and with whom you did it. Get the reader's attention.

DETAILS Add details to help your reader see, hear, and feel what happened. What did you and your friend say? Was anything funny?

MIDDLE Decide which events to include. You can organize these events later. For now, just write down the important things that you remember.

ENDING Think of how you want to end the narrative. Your ending should tell how the project turned out and how you felt about it.

Beginning	Details
I built a snow penguin with my friend Linda last year.	We had two feet of snow.
Middle **Events:** • We worked all morning. • The penguin was so tall, we couldn't reach the top. • Linda had the idea of making the penguin lying down. • We knocked down the penguin.	My mom gave us hot chocolate when we got cold. Linda said, "Let's push him over." The penguin broke into a hundred pieces.
Ending Linda said we should rebuild.	We decided to have more hot chocolate first. Then I was ready to rebuild.

Try It!

Use a Graphic Organizer to Get Started

Now use the events chart below to gather ideas for the beginning, middle, and ending for your own personal narrative.

Beginning	Details
Middle Events to include:	
Ending	

2. Organize

You are almost ready to begin a draft of your personal narrative. You can use a graphic organizer to help organize the events and details you gathered during brainstorming. You can also use the graphic organizer as you work through the different parts of your draft. The writer of the mentor text completed this graphic organizer.

BEGINNING In the first paragraph, you

- tell the topic of your personal narrative
- explain when and with whom you did the project

MIDDLE In the middle of the narrative, you

- describe what happened
- include dialogue and lively details

ENDING Your ending should

- show how the project turned out
- tell how you felt about it

Beginning
I built a giant snowman with my best friend, Linda. It turned into a snow penguin.

Middle: Event 1
We worked all morning. The snow penguin got taller than we were. It was too tall to finish.

Middle: Event 2
We decided to make the penguin lie down, to look as if it were swimming.

Middle: Event 3
We pushed the penguin over, and it broke.

Ending
We decided to rebuild the snow penguin but to have some hot chocolate first. Then I was ready to fix the penguin.

Try It! Organize

Now use the graphic organizer below to organize the ideas and details you want to include in the different parts of your draft.

Beginning

Middle: Event 1

Middle: Event 2

Middle: Event 3

Ending

3. Draft

Now it is time to begin the first draft of your personal narrative. Remember, your draft does not have to be perfect! Use your notes, get your ideas down, and have fun. You will have time to make changes later. Start by drafting your narrative on a computer or on a separate sheet of paper. Tell about the project you and your friend worked on and how it turned out.

Writer's Craft: Using Time-Order Words and Phrases

Time-order words and phrases tell when something happened. They connect events to each other and tell in what order they happened. Here are some common time-order words and phrases that help to link events in a narrative.

Time-order words	first, next, then, when, while, before, after, later, during, last, meanwhile, finally
Time-order phrases	on the first day, all morning, after a while, a few days later, last year, later that afternoon, at the same time, at the end

The author of the mentor text uses time-order words and phrases in the second paragraph.

TIME-ORDER WORDS AND PHRASES Read this section of the mentor text. Circle the time-order words in the paragraph. Underline the time-order phrases.

> We worked all morning on our creation. When we got cold, we went inside to warm up. My mom gave us hot chocolate and then we headed back outside to continue building. After a couple of hours, we had gotten halfway up the penguin's body. The penguin was taller than we were. It was impossible to finish it!

Try It!

Write Your First Draft

On a computer or a separate sheet of paper, continue the draft of your personal narrative. Remember to use time-order words and phrases to show when the events happened. Use this drafting checklist to help you as you write.

✔ A good beginning gets your reader's attention. You can begin with a question, a statement, or any interesting or funny detail.

✔ In the beginning, explain what you did and with whom you did it.

✔ Tell events in the order in which they happened.

✔ Use time-order words or phrases to show when events happened.

✔ Include descriptive details and dialogue.

✔ At the end, tell how the project turned out and how you felt about it. Try to include a detail in the ending that your readers will remember.

Tips for Getting Started

• Talk with your friend about the project. Your friend might remember some details that you have forgotten.

• Brainstorm key phrases and ideas before you begin writing. Just write down the first details and ideas that come into your mind. This is a great warm-up to get you started!

• In a personal narrative, your feelings are especially important, so remember how you felt about the project. Jot down what you remember best. You can fill in with details when you revise and edit later.

4. Peer Review

After you finish your draft, work with a partner to review each other's work. Here is a draft of the mentor text. Read it with your partner. Together, answer the questions in the boxes. On the next page, you will see what the writer's classmate said about the draft.

BEGINNING In her draft, the writer does not explain what the weather was like. Why would this be a good detail to add?

_____

_____

MIDDLE The second paragraph could use some time-order words and phrases that link the events and show when things happened. What time-order words or phrases could you add to the second paragraph?

_____

_____

ENDING The ending does not show the writer's feelings. How did the writer feel about the project?

_____

_____

_____

An Early Draft:

The Day We Built a Snow Penguin

I have a great memory that I will remember my whole life. I built a giant snowman with my best friend, Linda. Well, it wasn't actually a snowman. It was a snow penguin.

We worked hard on the snow penguin. It was really cold outside, and we went inside to warm up. My mom gave us hot chocolate, and we headed back out to keep building. Soon the penguin was taller than we were. "We'll never reach to the top," I said. We had only finished halfway up the penguin's body.

"How are we going to make the head?" asked Linda.

"I don't know," I told her.

"I have an idea!" she said. "Let's push him over and make him lying down on his back. That way we will be able to reach all of him."

"Okay," I said. "Let's do it."

We stood in front of the penguin, counted to three, and then pushed him over. Instead of just lying on his back, the penguin fell into a hundred pieces. We stood and stared at the penguin for several minutes.

"Okay," said Linda. "We can rebuild him."

"Okay," I said.

"But first, maybe we should go in for another cup of hot chocolate," she said.

Then we went outside and fixed the penguin.

An Example Peer Review Form

This peer review form gives an example of how a classmate evaluated the draft of the mentor text shown on the previous page.

The beginning tells what the project is, who is there, and when it happens.	You did a good job of letting the reader know your feelings about the project.
The writer's feelings about the project are clear.	You could improve your personal narrative by explaining when this project happened.

The writer presents events in the order in which they happened.	You did a good job of writing events in the order in which they happened. You also included some interesting dialogue.
The writer includes interesting details and dialogue.	You could improve your personal narrative by adding some details that show what the snow penguin looked like.

The writer uses time-order words and phrases to show when events happened.	You did a good job of using time-order words and phrases to show when things happened.
	You could improve your personal narrative by adding more time-order words and phrases to paragraph 2.

The writer tells how the project turned out or adds a detail that readers will remember.	You did a good job of adding the detail about drinking hot chocolate before rebuilding the snow penguin. You told how the project turned out.
The ending includes the writer's feelings about the project.	You could improve your personal narrative by adding a sentence that tells your feelings about the project.

Try It!   **Peer Review with a Partner**

Now you are going to work with a partner to review each other's personal narrative drafts. You will use the peer review form below. If you need help, look back at the mentor text writer's peer review form for suggestions.

The beginning tells what the project is, who was there, and when it happened. **The writer's feelings about the project are clear.**	You did a good job of You could improve your personal narrative by
The writer presents events in the order in which they happened. **The writer includes interesting details and dialogue.**	You did a good job of You could improve your personal narrative by
The writer uses time-order words and phrases to show when events happened.	You did a good job of You could improve your personal narrative by
The writer tells how the project turned out or adds a detail that readers will remember. **The ending includes the writer's feelings about the project.**	You did a good job of You could improve your personal narrative by

Try It! Record Key Peer Review Comments

Now it's time for you and your partner to share your comments with each other. Listen to your partner's feedback, and write down the key comments in the left column. Then write some ideas for improving your draft in the right column.

My review says that my beginning	I will
My review says that the middle section	I will
My review says that my ending	I will

Use the space below to write anything else you notice about your draft that you think you can improve.

5. Revise

In this step of the writing process, you work on the parts of your draft that need improvement. Use the peer review form that your classmate completed to help you. Also use your own ideas about how to improve each part of your personal narrative. The checklist below includes some things to think about as you get ready to revise.

Revision Checklist

✔ Does my beginning catch the reader's interest? Do I explain what the project is and when and with whom I did this project?

✔ Are events presented in the order in which they happened?

✔ Do I use details, facts, and dialogue to explain this project?

✔ Is my ending interesting? Have I included my feelings?

✔ Do I use time-order words and phrases to show when the events happened?

✔ Do I use sensory language to share my experience with the reader?

Writer's Craft: Using Sensory Language

Adding sensory details makes your personal experience more real. For example, if you write about flying a kite, you may remember the sun in your eyes and the wind in your hair. Now look at the mentor text for examples of sensory language.

SENSORY LANGUAGE
Sensory language helps the reader see, smell, touch, taste, or hear elements of the story. Underline the sensory language in this part of the mentor text.

I felt glad that Linda still wanted to work on the penguin with me. But my mittens were wet, and my feet felt like icicles. I didn't want to start all over again.

Then Linda said, "I know. Let's have another cup of hot chocolate first."

What a great idea! The hot chocolate was like an electric blanket for my insides.

Try It!   Revise Your Personal Narrative

Checking for sensory details is an important part of revising a personal narrative. The paragraph below needs some sensory language. Fill in the blank spaces with details that appeal to the senses. Then compare your work with a partner.

> Last summer, my friend Jan and I made a kite. The kite was pretty, with a colorful tail that _____. The tail had _____, red, and _____ ribbons on it.
>
> We flew the kite on the beach. The wind was strong and _____. The sand was _____. My friend and I ran up and down the beach. The kite rose high into the air. It looked like a giant butterfly!

Writing Assignment

Now it's time to revise the draft of your personal narrative. Continue working on a computer or on a separate sheet of paper. Review the assignment below and the checklist to remember what to include.

> Think of a project that you worked on with a friend. Choose something you enjoyed. Why was the project important to you? Was it helpful to work with a friend? How did the project turn out? Did anything funny happen? What did you learn? What would you like to share about the experience with an audience?
>
> Write three to five paragraphs describing the project you and your friend worked on. Get your readers interested in your experience!

6. Edit

After revising your personal narrative, you will edit it. When you edit, you read very carefully to find any mistakes. Here's a checklist of some things to look for as you edit.

Editing Checklist

✔ Did you indent each paragraph?

✔ Are all of your sentences complete? Does each have a subject and a verb?

✔ Did you begin each sentence with a capital letter?

✔ Does each sentence end with the correct punctuation?

✔ Have you used quotation marks correctly in dialogue?

✔ Are all of your words spelled correctly?

You can use these editing marks to mark any errors you find.

> ⌃ Add   ⌄ Add a comma   ⌄⌄ Add quotation marks
> ↵ Add an apostrophe   ~~delete~~ Delete

These paragraphs from an early draft of the mentor text show how to use editing marks.

> We stood in front of the snow penguin counted to three and then pushed him over. But instead of just ~~licing~~ *lying* on his back, the penguin fell into a hundred ~~peices~~ *pieces*.
>
> "Oh no I yelled. "He's broken!" We stared at the broken penguin for ~~for~~ several minutes.
>
> "Dont worry," said Linda. "We can rebuild him."

Language Focus: Punctuating Dialogue, Using Possessives, and Spelling Correctly

Use quotation marks at the beginning and at the end of a speaker's exact words. Put commas, periods, or other end punctuation inside the quotation marks. **Example:** "Let's build a snowman," I said. "You can help me."

Use an apostrophe and the letter *s* to show possession, or that something belongs to someone. **Examples:** Help me find Mario's mittens. Sometimes children's coats are left on the playground.

Use correct spelling when adding endings to words.

Many words are formed by adding *-ed* and *-ing* without any change. **Example:** wish, wished, wishing

For words ending in a silent *e*, drop the *e* before adding *-ed* or *-ing*. **Example:** like, liked, liking

For words ending in a consonant and *y*, change the *y* to *i* before adding *-ed*, but do not make any change before adding *-ing*. **Example:** spy, spied, spying

For words ending in a vowel and *y*, add *-ed* and *-ing* without making any other change. **Example:** play, played, playing

"How are we going to make its head?" asked Linda.

"I don't know," I told her. "We'll never reach to the top."

"I have an idea!" she said. "Let's push him over and make him lie down. He could look as if he's swimming on his back. That way we will be able to reach all parts of him."

"Great idea!" I said. "Let's do it."

PUNCTUATING DIALOGUE Read this section of the mentor text. Quotation marks show the exact words that a speaker says. Underline the dialogue in this part of the mentor text. Circle the words that tell you who the speakers are.

Try It! Language and Editing Practice

Practice using correct punctuation. Find the punctuation mistakes in the following sentences. Correct the errors. Add any missing punctuation.

1. If you help me, we can build the snowman faster I said.

2. Where are my mittens? Have you seen them Mario asked.

3. Did you leave them in Sams house I asked

4. No, I had them with me a minute ago he said.

5. Look They're in the snowman! I exclaimed.

Now use editing marks to correct the errors in this paragraph:

What kind of snowman shall we make" I asked"

"I want to make a snow goose Leo replyed.

"How do you make a snow goose I asked.

"It is not difficult to make Leo said. But we need two big sticks for its legs" he added.

There are some big sticks in Teds yard I said Maybe he will let us use them

Try It!   Edit Your Personal Narrative

Now edit your personal narrative. Use this checklist and the editing marks you have learned to correct any errors you find.

- ☐ Are all of your sentences complete? Does each have a subject and a verb?

- ☐ Did you begin each sentence with a capital letter?

- ☐ Does each sentence end with the correct punctuation?

- ☐ Have you used possessives correctly?

- ☐ Have you used correct punctuation for dialogue? Are commas used correctly?

- ☐ Are all of your words spelled correctly?

Editing Tips

- Read your writing aloud to yourself or a classmate. This will help you find missing words and awkward phrases. Ask yourself, "Does that sound right?"

- As you read, listen carefully for stops and pauses. Stops and pauses usually are places where punctuation should go. Ask yourself, "Am I missing any commas? Should I add a question mark?"

- Read your writing over slowly at least two times. When looking for errors, one reading is not enough!

 Publish

On a computer or a separate sheet of paper, make a neat final draft of your personal narrative. Correct all errors that you found while editing your draft. Be sure to give your personal narrative a good title!

The final step is to publish your personal narrative. Here are some different ways you might share your work.

- Illustrate your writing with drawings or photographs.

- Read your personal narrative aloud to the class. If possible, do a joint reading with the friend who shared your project.

- Gather your personal narrative and the work of your classmates into a booklet.

- Create a bulletin board display with your personal narratives.

Technology Suggestions

- Upload your personal narrative onto your class or school blog.
- Print out your personal narrative using decorative borders or paper.
- Send your personal narrative as an e-mail to the friend who worked on the project with you.

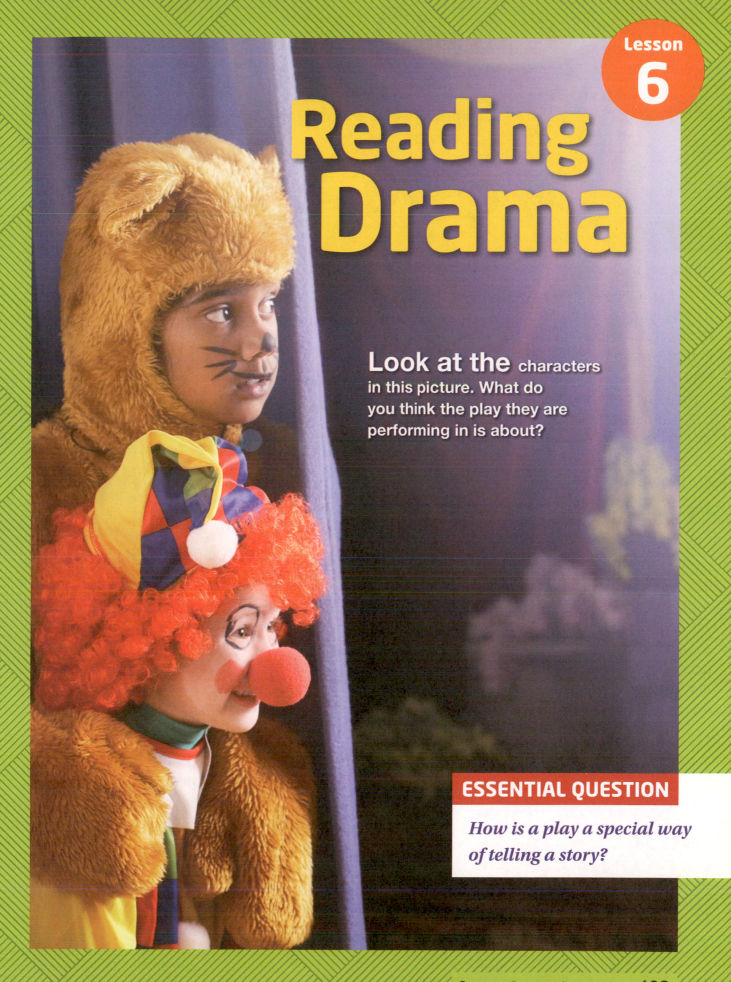

Reading Drama

Look at the characters in this picture. What do you think the play they are performing in is about?

ESSENTIAL QUESTION

How is a play a special way of telling a story?

Consider ▶ Can a selfish person become kind and generous?

Can things you imagine make a difference in the real world?

A Garden to Share

Cast of Characters

Marcus and Alma, nine-year-old twins

Mrs. Jinn, an unexpected visitor

Mom, the twins' mother

Mr. Grump, the landlord

Scene 1

SETTING: An apartment in a large building in a city. The childen are sitting on the floor in Alma's bedroom.

1   **Marcus:** What's that?

Alma: Just an old bottle. I found it in the empty lot.

Marcus: What do you want that for? It's old junk, like everything else in this city!

Alma: Ever since we moved here, all you do is complain.

5   **Marcus:** I don't like it here. I want to go back to Grandpa's farm.

Alma: *(sighs)* I miss the farm, too. I wish we could clean up the empty lot and make a garden.

Marcus: Our mean landlord said to stay out of that lot. *(mockingly)* The trash is dangerous, he says. Better watch out for that old bottle!

Alma: Sometimes old glass is really valuable. I'm going to clean it up.

(*Alma polishes the bottle. Suddenly there is a loud knock. The door flies open, and Mrs. Jinn bursts in. Her odd clothing is covered with sparkles.*)

Alma and Marcus: (*both jumping up*) Who are you?

10 **Mrs. Jinn:** Hee-hee! I have surprised you. How enchanting! You know, it is getting harder and harder to surprise people, especially grown-ups. Nothing surprises them! Who am I? My name is Mrs. Jinn.

Alma: What are you doing here?

Mrs. Jinn: Hee-hee. I have come to assist you. I love assisting people! You want to make a garden in the empty lot. You want to grow beautiful flowers and delicious vegetables. You loved your grandfather's farm. You want to turn the empty lot into a little piece of the farm you loved. How enchanting!

Marcus: How do you know all this? We've never laid eyes on you!

Mrs. Jinn: I know many things. I know your landlord, Mr. Grump. He is not a bad man, but he is worried. He thinks making a garden is too much work for you.

SEQUENCE The sequence of events is the order in which things happen. At the start of the play, Marcus and Alma talk about moving to the city—an event that happened before the play begins. What event involving the landlord do they mention that happened before the start of the play?

DIALOGUE The words characters speak are called dialogue. In drama, a character name appears before each line of dialogue to tell the reader which character is speaking. What the characters say can show what they are thinking, feeling, or doing. What can you tell about Mrs. Jinn from what she says in the dialogue?

CHARACTER TRAITS Character traits are the details about characters that show what they are like. Mrs. Jinn laughs a lot. This character trait tells you that she is a cheerful person. What character trait does Mrs. Jinn say Mr. Grump has?

NONLITERAL LANGUAGE
Sometimes words mean something different from what they actually say. This is called nonliteral language. When Marcus says the children have never "laid eyes" on Mrs. Jinn, he does not mean they never put their eyes on top of her. He means they have never seen her. When Mrs. Jinn says Mr. Grump will "change his tune," she does not mean he will start singing a different song. What does she mean?

15 **Marcus:** Too much work? He should see the garden we had at Grandpa's farm! Alma, show her the photographs. Maybe she can show Mr. Grump what we did.

(Alma goes to the desk, picks up several photographs, and shows them to Mrs. Jinn.)

Mrs. Jinn: Oh, wonderful! I will take these to Mr. Grump. He will change his tune! *(to Alma)* Be careful with that bottle.

(Mrs. Jinn goes out the door. The door opens again, and Mom looks in.)

Mom: Hey, kids, time for lunch.

Alma: Mom, who was that lady?

Mom: What lady?

20 **Marcus:** Mrs. Jinn—that lady with the sparkly clothes.

Mom: I didn't see anyone. You and your imaginations!

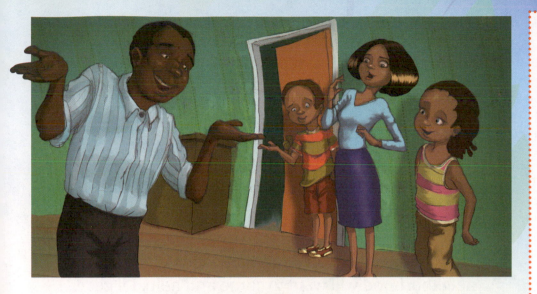

Scene 2

SETTING: *Living room of the apartment. Mom, Marcus, Alma, and Mr. Grump are having a conversation.*

Mom: Thank you for coming to talk with us, Mr. Grump.

Mr. Grump: It's my pleasure. What a wonderful idea it is to make a garden! I will pay for all the tools and seeds. I can't wait to see the empty lot exploding with pretty flowers instead of all that old trash.

Mom: Why, Mr. Grump, that's very nice of you. What made you change your mind?

25   **Mr. Grump:** *(seeming dazed)* Well, I thought making a garden would be too hard for the children. But I think I had a dream about it. A woman came to talk to me—a very cheerful woman wearing sparkly clothes. She showed me pictures of the garden Marcus and Alma used to have and said they would work really hard. You know, she made me feel cheerful. And she convinced me that a garden would be just the thing to improve my building. I can see now that she was right about Marcus and Alma. I can see that they really will work hard. *(to the children)* Any help you need, just let me know. *(Mr. Grump leaves.)*

DRAMA: SCENES Plays are often divided into parts called scenes. A new scene starts when the setting changes. The scene may bring new characters or information into the story. A long play may have several scenes grouped into sections called acts. In Scene 2, Mr. Grump appears in the play for the first time. What is surprising about what he says?

MAKE INFERENCES When you make an inference, you use clues in the text and what you already know to figure out something that is not directly stated in the text. Mr. Grump says he thinks he had a dream about a funny lady in sparkling clothes. What inference can you make about what may have happened?

ASK AND ANSWER QUESTIONS In Scene 1, you read that Mr. Grump told the children to stay out of the empty lot. But at the start of Scene 2, he says making the garden is a wonderful idea. What question could you ask yourself about Mr. Grump at this point in the play?

Mom: What happened to Mr. Grump? He's always been grumpy, and suddenly he's so positive. Isn't that amazing?

Marcus: Yes. It's amazing!

Mom: *(puzzled)* By the way, didn't you kids mention a lady in sparkly clothes?

30 **Alma and Marcus:** Did we?

Mom: Well, anyway, put your jackets on so we can go to the store and get the tools and seeds. This is going to be fun! I bet all the kids in the neighborhood will want to come and help. I'll get my purse and see you at the car.

(Mom goes out the door, and Mrs. Jinn comes in.)

Mrs. Jinn: You see, Mr. Grump isn't so mean at all. Now you can make your garden, and Mr. Grump will even help you. Oh, how enchanting!

Marcus: What did you do? How did you make Mr. Grump change like that?

Mrs. Jinn: I just helped him to feel more cheerful. And I helped him see that a having a garden would improve the building he owns. I was so happy to assist him!

Alma: How can we thank you?

35 **Mrs. Jinn:** Oh, no need to thank me. But—can you give me that bottle back?

Alma: Oh, is it yours? I thought it was just old trash. *(gives her the bottle)*

Mrs. Jinn: Oh yes, my dear. Quite right. Old trash. Good-bye. So enchanting to assist you! Hee-hee! *(She goes out the door.)*

Marcus: Amazing!

Alma: You might even say enchanting!

POINT OF VIEW The old bottle plays an important part in the story. How do you think Alma feels about the bottle? Do you think the old bottle is special in any way?

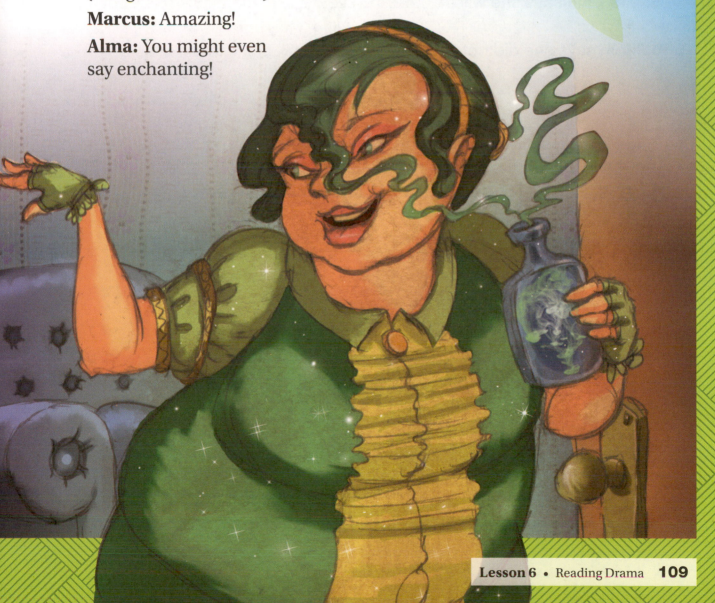

Comprehension Check

Think about the sequence of events in "A Garden to Share." Then complete the following sentences to summarize the events in the play.

Scene 1

1. Marcus asks _____ about the bottle.

2. Marcus and Alma talk about wanting to _____.

3. Alma starts to polish _____.

4. _____ bursts in the door.

5. Mrs. Jinn says she will _____.

6. Mom says she did not _____.

Scene 2

7. Mr. Grump says he will help _____.

8. _____ says he changed his mind because _____

_____

_____.

9. Mom is puzzled because _____.

10. _____ comes back.

11. _____ gives Mrs. Jinn _____.

12. _____ leaves with the bottle.

Vocabulary

Use the word map below to help you define and use one of the highlighted vocabulary words from the Share and Learn reading or another word your teacher assigns you.

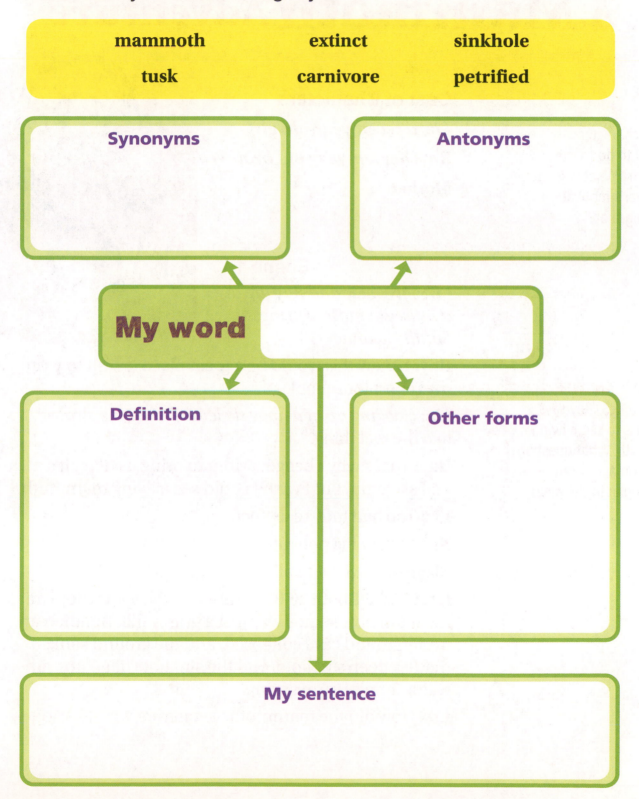

mammoth   extinct   sinkhole

tusk   carnivore   petrified

Synonyms

Antonyms

My word

Definition

Other forms

My sentence

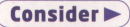
Consider ▶ What was the world like thousands of years ago?

How do people today learn about the distant past?

A Mammoth Adventure

DIALOGUE
Which character wanted to go to the museum? What was the character's motivation for doing that?

_____

_____

_____

ASK AND ANSWER QUESTIONS Ray says he wants to see a living mammoth. What question could you ask about what will happen in the play?

_____

_____

_____

Cast of Characters

Liz, a seven-year-old girl

Ray, her ten-year-old brother

Mother

Scene 1

SETTING: Liz and Ray are at a museum in Hot Springs, South Dakota.

1   **Ray:** I knew this would be a great place to visit to write my report for school.

Liz: *(looking up at a huge skeleton)* Wow! It's almost like the real thing.

Ray: That's why I begged Mom to bring us here. It's a real skeleton! But I wish I could see a living mammoth.

Liz: Too bad they're extinct.

5   **Ray:** A very big pool of warm water used to be here.

Liz: Is that why it's called Hot Springs?

Ray: Right. About 26,000 years ago, the spot where this museum now stands was just a grassy hill. But then an underground cave collapsed, and the ground sank. It made a deep sinkhole, and the sinkhole filled up with water from a warm spring.

Liz: How did the mammoths get here?

Ray: The water was warm all year round. Lots of mammoths and other animals went into the pool to drink, but then they couldn't get out. The sides were too steep. So the animals died, either because they drowned or because they couldn't get food.

10 **Liz:** Where is the water now?

Ray: The pool slowly filled up with dirt. The bones of the trapped animals were protected under the mud for thousands and thousands of years. Now people are digging them out. There were about fifty mammoths trapped here, and lots of other animals, like wolves, and camels, and a giant bear.

Liz: The poor animals! I feel sorry for them, trapped like that. I wouldn't want to be there!

Ray: I would. I'd give my right arm to see all those mammoths alive. I could use Mom's cell phone to take a picture. Wow, my school report on mammoths would be awesome!

Liz: Yeah, you'd get an A as long as you didn't get trapped in the pool.

15 **Ray:** Here—look at this! *(Ray goes to a diagram that is hanging on a nearby wall. The diagram has a sign that says "Please do not touch." Ray reads from it.)* This diagram shows what happened to the mammoths through the years. *(He points to the first part of the diagram. It has a label that says "26,000 years ago.")* That's when the ground caved in and made the pool.

NONLITERAL LANGUAGE What does Ray mean when he says "I'd give my right arm" to see the mammoths alive?

_____

_____

_____

SEQUENCE What events led to finding the mammoth bones at Hot Springs? List the sequence of events Ray describes in the dialogue.

_____

_____

_____

CHARACTER TRAITS Liz says she feels sorry for the animals that were trapped in the sinkhole. What does this tell you about Liz's character?

_____

_____

_____

SEQUENCE OF EVENTS
What event happens right before Ray says "Hey, what's happening?"

_____

_____

_____

MAKE INFERENCES
After Liz and Ray fall to the ground, what has changed about their surroundings? What inference can you make about what has happened?

_____

_____

_____

Liz: There's when the mammoths died in the water! (_Liz reaches out and touches the picture of a mammoth on the diagram._)

Ray: Hey, what's happening? What's that noise?

Liz: I don't know—I can't see anything! I feel like I'm falling!

(_Liz and Ray pretend to tumble through the air and fall to the ground._)

Scene 2

Ray: What happened?

20 **Liz:** Where's the museum?

Ray: Where are we?

Liz: It's just a grassy hill. And there's some snow on the ground, too. And there's a giant something . . . it looks all furry . . . oh no, what is that?

Ray: Well, if it looks like an elephant but it has long, brown fur . . .

Liz: . . . and big, sharp tusks that curve at the ends . . .

25 **Ray:** It's a woolly mammoth!

(Liz and Ray begin to walk backward together, very slowly.)

Liz: We must have traveled back in time to the Ice Age! *(She looks scared.)* Are mammoths <mark>carnivores</mark>?

Ray: They don't eat meat. *(Suddenly, Ray looks scared, too. He points in a different direction.)* But that giant bear definitely does!

Liz: And it's coming this way!

Ray: What's happening to the ground? It's starting to shake! And look, there's a crack opening up!

30 **Liz:** Oh, no! It's starting to make a sinkhole!

Ray: Quick—draw a big square in the snow!

Liz: With what?

Ray: Your finger, your finger!

(Liz uses her finger to draw a big square on the ground.)

Liz: Okay—now what?

35 **Ray:** Use your finger to write the year inside the square.

Liz: What year?

Ray: The year we were in before this happened. Hurry!

CONTEXT CLUES Which words in the dialogue help you understand what the word <mark>carnivores</mark> means? Circle them.

MOTIVATION At the beginning of the play, Ray says he wants to see a living mammoth. Do you think he still has the same motivation at this point in the drama? Explain.

_____

_____

_____

DRAMA: SCENES What happens in the second scene that makes the story more exciting?

_____

_____

_____

NONLITERAL LANGUAGE An ice age can last for thousands years. Does Liz think that it would take thousands of years to explain to her mother where she and Ray were? Is Liz using literal or nonliteral language?

MAKE INFERENCES Why do you think Liz and Ray don't tell their mother about their adventure?

POINT OF VIEW How do Liz and Ray feel about their adventure? How would you feel if you could travel back in time? What things would you like to see?

(Liz writes the date, and she and Ray stand inside the square. Once again they seem to tumble through the air and fall to the ground.)

Liz: We're back in the museum!

Ray: What a relief!

40 **Liz:** That was close.

(Their Mother enters.)

Mother: What happened to you two? I couldn't find you for a minute! I got the tickets for the dinosaur show later, but it's lunchtime now. Where did you two go?

Liz: What's for lunch? I hope it's not mammoth!

Ray: We almost *were* lunch.

Mother: Huh? What are you talking about?

45 **Ray:** I was petrified.

Mother: Petrified! What frightened you?

Liz: Oh . . . I think it would take an Ice Age to explain it. Let's go have lunch. *(Ray and Liz giggle.)*

Anchor Standard Discussion Question

Discuss the following question with your peer group. Then record your answer in the space provided.

1. How are the events in Scene 1 of "A Mammoth Adventure" different from the events in Scene 2? Which scene do you find more interesting, and why? Support your answers with details from the play.

_____

_____

_____

_____

_____

_____

_____

_____

_____

_____

_____

Comprehension Check

1. Do you think Ray's visit to the museum will help him write a good report for school? Explain.

_____

_____

_____

2. "A Mammoth Adventure" includes both a real adventure and a fantasy adventure. Explain what the real adventure is, and then explain the adventure that is fantasy.

_____

_____

_____

3. What question is never answered in "A Mammoth Adventure"? Would the play be better if it answered this question? Explain.

_____

_____

_____

Read On Your Own

Read another drama, "Attic Stardust," independently. Apply what you learned in this lesson and check your understanding.

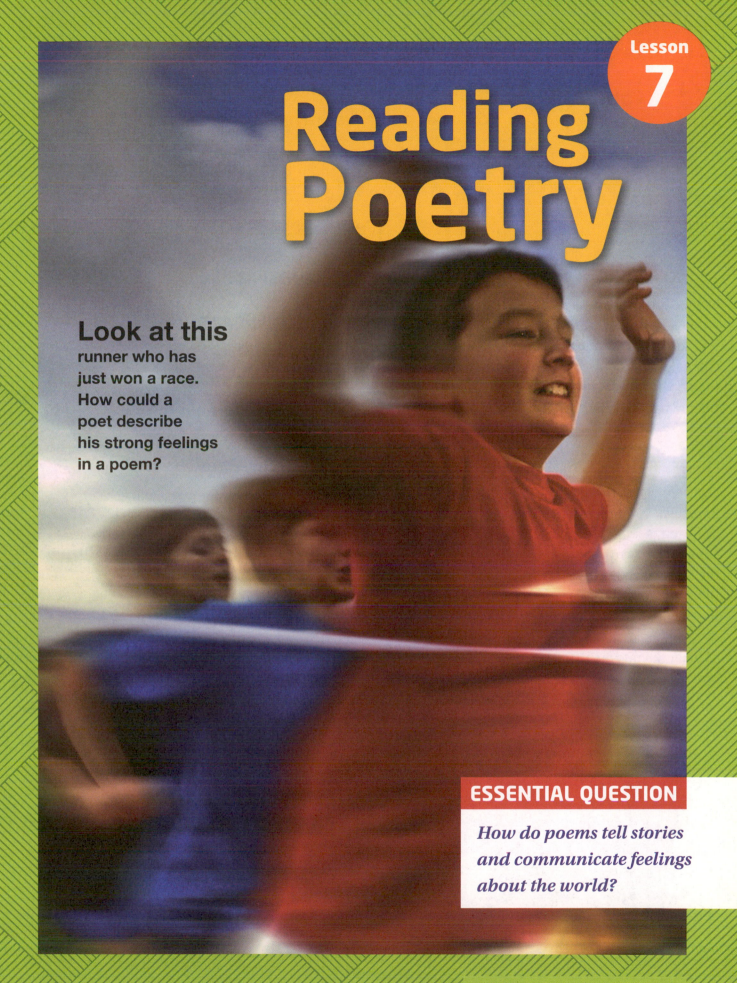

Reading Poetry

Look at this runner who has just won a race. How could a poet describe his strong feelings in a poem?

ESSENTIAL QUESTION

How do poems tell stories and communicate feelings about the world?

Consider ▶ How is a poem different from a story?

How does poetry use rhyme and rhythm to tell a story?

POETRY Poetry uses carefully chosen words to express ideas and feelings or to tell a story. Rhyme, rhythm, and colorful descriptions are characteristics of poetry. How does the poet describe the town of Hamelin?

CONTEXT CLUES Context clues are words near an unfamiliar word that give clues to the word's meaning. Look at the word *vermin* in the last line on this page. What is the first word on the next page? Read the description on the next page of what the rats do. These are clues. What does the word *vermin* mean?

from
The Pied Piper of Hamelin

by Robert Browning

1   Hamelin Town's in Brunswick,
    By famous Hanover city;
    The River Weser, deep and wide,
    Washes its wall on the southern side;
5   A pleasanter spot you never spied;
    But, when begins my ditty,
    Almost five hundred years ago,
    To see the townsfolk suffer so
    From vermin, was a pity.

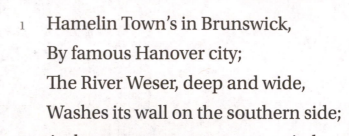

10 Rats!
   They fought the dogs and killed the cats,
   And bit the babies in the cradles,
   And ate the cheeses out of the vats,
   And licked the soup from the cook's own ladles,
15 Split open the kegs of salted sprats,[1]
   Made nests inside men's Sunday hats,
   And even spoiled the women's chats,
   By drowning their speaking
   With shrieking and squeaking
20 In fifty different sharps and flats.

[1] **sprats** small fish

RHYME Rhyme is the repeating of sounds at the ends of lines; for example, *speaking* and *squeaking*. Which lines on this page end in words that rhyme with *rats*?

RHYTHM Like music, poetry has a beat, or rhythm. Rhythm is the pattern of stressed and unstressed syllables you hear when the line is read aloud. Reread these lines, noting the rhythm: *Made **nests** in**side** men's **Sun**day **hats**, / And **even spoiled** the **wo**men's **chats**.* Now read the last three lines on this page out loud, emphasizing the rhythm. How does the rhythm of the poem support the story?

NONLITERAL LANGUAGE Poets often use words to say something different from what the words usually mean. Read how the rats shrieked and squeaked "in fifty different sharps and flats." Sharps and flats are types of musical notes. The rats are not really making music. They are just making a lot of noise. How does this description help you imagine the sounds of the rats?

ASK AND ANSWER QUESTIONS Asking yourself questions and looking for the answers as you read can help you understand what you are reading. As you read the first few lines of the poem, you might have asked, "Why would people in a pleasant town like Hamelin be suffering?" Then you find the answer as you read on—they suffer because of rats! What question might you ask when you finish reading the lines on this page?

CONTEXT CLUES The fact that the townspeople are angry with the mayor is a clue that the word *noddy* means "a foolish person." Reread the last three lines on this page for clues to the meaning of *dolts*. What do you think a dolt is? What context clues helped you determine that?

At last the people in a body
To the Town Hall came flocking:
"Tis clear," cried they, "our Mayor's a noddy;
And as for our Corporation[2]—shocking
25 To think we buy gowns lined with ermine[3]
For dolts that can't or won't determine
What's best to rid us of our vermin!

[2] **Corporation** leaders of the town
[3] **ermine** white fur of a winter weasel

STANZAS In a narrative poem, events are usually organized in stanzas. The stanzas on these pages are taken from a longer poem. Each stanza builds on earlier stanzas to tell the story and create suspense to keep the reader's attention. These stanzas present the problem of the people of Hamelin. What is the problem? What do you think will happen next?

You hope, because you're old and obese,
To find in the furry civic⁴ robe ease?
30 Rouse⁵ up, sirs! Give your brains a racking⁶
To find the remedy we're lacking,
Or, sure as fate, we'll send you packing!"
At this the Mayor and Corporation
Quaked with a mighty consternation.

⁴ **civic** having to do with a city

⁵ **Rouse** wake up

⁶ **racking** stretching

CONTEXT CLUES In the lines on this page, the townspeople threaten to send the mayor "packing," and then the mayor and the corporation "quaked." Why are the mayor and his corporation quaking? How are they feeling? How does this help you understand what *consternation* means?

Comprehension Check

Look back at the excerpt from "The Pied Piper of Hamelin" to see how the poet describes the town of Hamelin and its people. Draw conclusions by looking closely at the poet's words. Answer the questions below with details from the poem.

A. Are the events in the poem real or imaginary?	**How can you tell?**
The events are imaginary.	The description sounds like a fairy tale. The illustrations are funny, not scary.
B. What does the poet think of the rats?	**How can you tell?**
C. What do the people in the town think about the leaders in charge?	**Why do they think that?**
D. How do the leaders feel at the end of this section of the poem?	**Why do they feel that way?**

Vocabulary

Use the word map below to help you define and use one of the highlighted vocabulary words from the Share and Learn reading or another word your teacher assigns you.

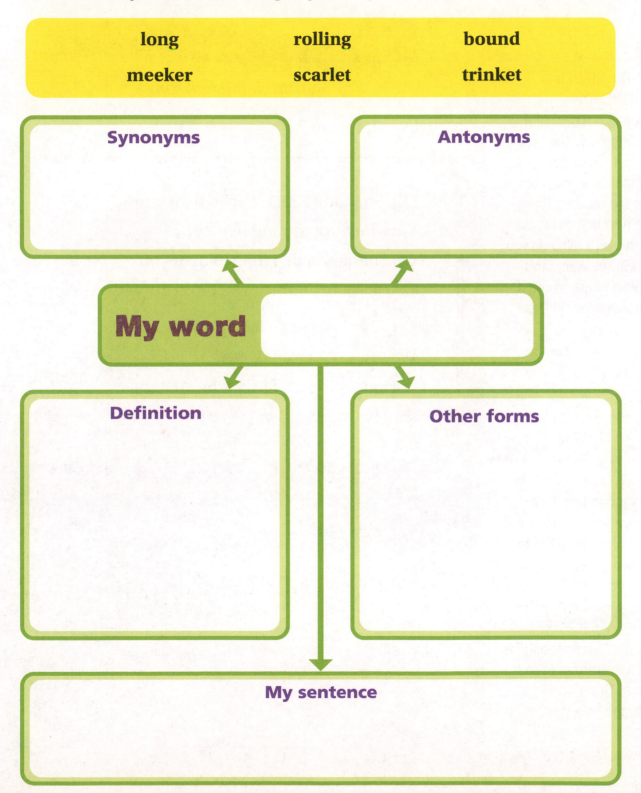

long	rolling	bound
meeker	scarlet	trinket

Synonyms

Antonyms

My word

Definition

Other forms

My sentence

Consider ▶ How do songs and poems express the feelings of their creators?

How are poems and songs alike or similar?

Shenandoah

a traditional folk song

ASK AND ANSWER QUESTIONS The Shenandoah is a beautiful river in Virginia. In the 1800s, some people from the Shenandoah area moved west, crossing the Missouri River to make new homes on the American plains. Who do you think is the speaker in this song? What question could you ask about the speaker?

_____

_____

_____

CONTEXT CLUES Find the word bound in line 4. Which words give you a clue to the meaning of *bound*? Circle those words, and draw an arrow to *bound*.

STANZAS "Shenandoah" is arranged in stanzas of four lines each. Draw a line to separate the two stanzas on this page.

1 Oh, Shenandoah, I long to hear you,
Way-hey, you rolling river.
Oh Shenandoah, I long to hear you
Cause we're bound away 'cross the wide Missouri.

5 Oh, Shenandoah, I love your daughter
Way-hey, you rolling river.
Oh Shenandoah, I love your daughter
And we're bound away 'cross the wide Missouri.

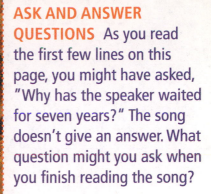

ASK AND ANSWER QUESTIONS As you read the first few lines on this page, you might have asked, "Why has the speaker waited for seven years?" The song doesn't give an answer. What question might you ask when you finish reading the song?

_____

_____

_____

For seven years I waited for her.
10 Way-hey, you rolling river.
For seven years, I waited for her,
And we're bound away 'cross the wide Missouri.

Farewell, my dear, I'm bound to leave you.
Way-hey, you rolling river.
15 Farewell, my dear, I'm bound to leave you,
And we're bound away 'cross the wide Missouri.

STANZAS The first line of each stanza in this song adds a detail to a story that builds on the earlier details. What do you think the song is about?

_____

_____

_____

REPETITION Each stanza of the song has lines that are repeated in other stanzas. Why do you think these lines are repeated? How does the repetition help build the story the song is telling?

_____

_____

_____

The Wind

by Robert Louis Stevenson

ASK AND ANSWER QUESTIONS At the start of the poem, you might ask yourself, "Who is the poet talking to?" Circle the lines that tell the answer.

NONLITERAL LANGUAGE
Look at line 4. The poem is comparing the soft sound of the wind to the sound of ladies' long skirts brushing across the grass. How are these two things similar?

_____

_____

_____

1 I saw you toss the kites on high
  And blow the birds about the sky;
  And all around I heard you pass,
  Like ladies' skirts across the grass—
5 O wind, a-blowing all day long!
  O wind, that sings so loud a song!

  I saw the different things you did,
  But always you yourself you hid.
  I felt you push, I heard you call,
10 I could not see yourself at all—
  O wind, a-blowing all day long,
  O wind, that sings so loud a song!

O you that are so strong and cold,

O blower, are you young or old?

15 Are you a beast of field and tree,

Or just a stronger child than me?

O wind, a-blowing all day long,

O wind, that sings so loud a song!

NONLITERAL LANGUAGE
Look at line 15. How can the wind be a beast?

_____

_____

_____

DESCRIPTION The poet wonders what the wind might be. Underline the descriptions of the wind the poet wonders about.

_____

_____

_____

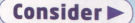 **Consider** ▶ How can a poem describe a season of the year?

How does the poet feel about autumn?

Autumn

by Emily Dickinson

ASK AND ANSWER QUESTIONS One question you might ask yourself is, "What does the poet mean by 'the rose is out of town'?" How would you answer this question?

_____

_____

_____

NONLITERAL LANGUAGE The poem says that in the fall, the maple tree wears a bright scarf and the field wears a red gown. What is the poet really describing?

_____

_____

_____

RHYMING Which words in this poem rhyme? Circle the words.

The morns are meeker than they were,
The nuts are getting brown;
The berry's cheek is plumper,
The rose is out of town.

The maple wears a gayer scarf,
The field a scarlet gown.
Lest I should be old-fashioned,
I'll put a trinket[1] on.

[1] **trinket** a small decoration

Anchor Standard Discussion Question

Discuss the following question with your peer group. Then record your answer in the space provided.

1. Why do you think the writers of "Shenandoah," "The Wind," and "Autumn" describe things in nature as if they are human beings? Support your answer with details from the texts.

_____

_____

_____

_____

_____

_____

_____

_____

_____

_____

_____

_____

_____

Comprehension Check

1. The song "Shenandoah" is about leaving something behind and moving to a new place. What is being left behind? Is the new place better than what is being left behind? Reread the song, and use details to support your answer.

_____

_____

_____

2. In "The Wind," the poet talks directly to the wind, although he cannot see the wind. How does he say he knows the wind is there? Use details from the poem to support your answer.

_____

_____

_____

3. Poets often use words to "paint" pictures. How does Emily Dickinson use words to paint a picture of autumn? Use details from the poem to support your answer.

_____

_____

_____

Read On Your Own

Read another poem independently. Apply what you learned in this lesson and check your understanding.

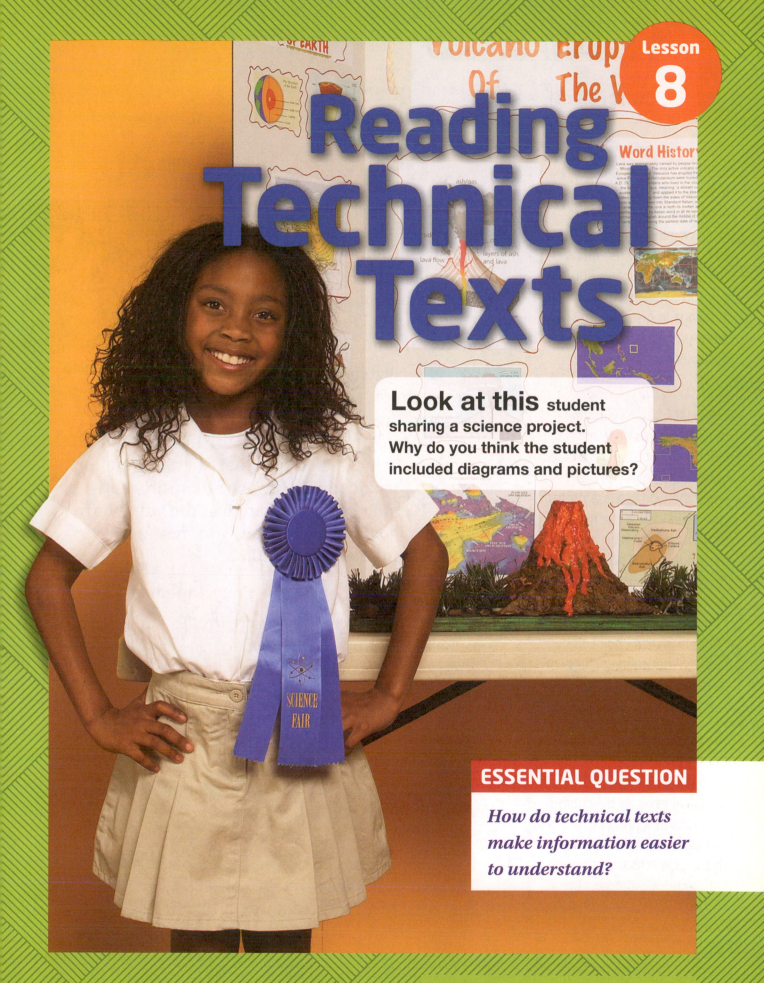

Reading Technical Texts

Look at this student sharing a science project. Why do you think the student included diagrams and pictures?

ESSENTIAL QUESTION

How do technical texts make information easier to understand?

Consider ▶

What is the Internet?

How do you use the Internet to find information?

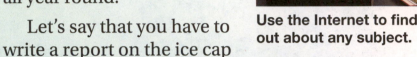

Using the Internet

Antarctica is the southernmost continent on Earth. The South Pole is located on Antarctica. It is so cold that a giant ice cap covers most of the continent all year round.

Use the Internet to find out about any subject.

Let's say that you have to write a report on the ice cap in Antarctica, and you head to a computer. One good source of information is the Internet. The Internet includes Web sites that offer information about a specific topic. However, there are many, many Web sites about Antarctica. You won't have time to read them all! So, start your research by using an online encyclopedia.

Step 1   **Search for Online Encyclopedias**

Open an Internet search engine. To find out about a subject, you need to use keywords. Keywords are words or phrases that describe information about the subject. A search engine will go through millions of Web sites looking for information that matches your keywords.

Type "encyclopedias" in the box in your search engine and click *Go*. The names of many different encyclopedias will appear on the screen. Find one you or your teacher know about. Click the link to it.

5   Look for a search box at the top of the page. Type "ice cap" into the search box and click *Go*. You will find a list of articles, pictures, and movies.

TECHNICAL TEXTS

Technical texts explain how to do something or how something works. They are often about science and technology. They use maps, charts, diagrams, photographs, steps in a process, and headings to give information. What process is explained in this selection?

CONTEXT CLUES

Context clues are words near an unknown word that give clues to its meaning. If you don't know the word *southernmost*, you could look at the next sentence, which tells you that the South Pole is on Antarctica. This can help you figure out that *southernmost* means "the farthest south." Look at the term *search engine* under Step 1. What context clues can help you figure out what this word means?

STEPS IN A PROCESS

Writers often organize technical texts by describing the steps in a process, or the stages of doing something. This article tells the steps in finding information on the Internet. What is the first step in this process?

Step 2 Narrow Your Search

When you want to know more about a topic, you can narrow your search. Perhaps you want to know more about the ice cap and Antarctica. First, look back at what you read in the encyclopedia. Then look for the underlined, colored word "Antarctica." This is a link. When you click it, a page about Antarctica will open. If you do not see a link, go back to the search box and type in "Antarctica."

Step 3 Find More Resources

An encyclopedia is not the only place to find information. You can find information on many kinds of Web sites. To practice using other kinds of Web sites, go back to your Internet search page. This time, type in the keywords "ice cap Antarctica."

Not all the information you find on the Internet is correct. So how do you know which links to trust? Look for Web pages written by experts. Experts are people who know a lot about a subject. Their Web addresses often end with *.gov*, *.org*, or *.edu*.

If you need help, ask your teacher or your school librarian. They can give you a list of Web sites about a subject. You can also look in a book. It might list some Web sites you can visit to find out more information. Turn to the next page to look at a trustworthy Web page about Antarctica.

Listen and Learn

SEQUENCE Sequence words help connect ideas in a text. Sequence words like *first*, *next*, and *last* tell you that the author is describing things in time order. What sequence words can you find in the first paragraph on this page? What do they tell you?

LABELS Labels are short explanations that identify a picture or photograph and its parts. Look at the map on this page. What are the labels on the map?

USE MAPS A map can help you understand where a place is in relation to other places. If you look at the map below, you can see that Antarctica is south of all the other continents of the world. Which bodies of water surround Antarctica? Which landmass is closest to Antarctica?

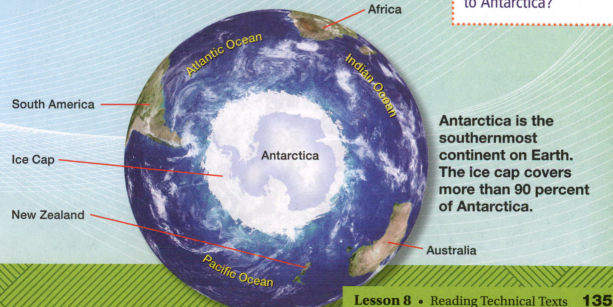

Africa
Atlantic Ocean
Indian Ocean
South America
Ice Cap
Antarctica
New Zealand
Australia
Pacific Ocean

Antarctica is the southernmost continent on Earth. The ice cap covers more than 90 percent of Antarctica.

USE PHOTOS Photographs can add more information to what is in the text. The photograph on this page shows what the ice cap of Antarctica looks like. How does this add information to what you have read in the text?

ASK AND ANSWER QUESTIONS Readers ask and answer questions about a text to show they understand what they are reading. Look at paragraph 12. What are the areas of bare rock in Antarctica called?

CAUSE AND EFFECT Cause and effect is the relationship that tells when one event causes another event to happen. The cause makes the effect happen, and the effect is what happens as a result. Look at the last paragraph on this page. What is the effect as an iceberg slowly drifts into warmer waters?

Antarctica

10 Antarctica, which is the southernmost continent on the planet, covers almost 5.5 million square miles. It is the fifth-largest continent in the world. The word *Antarctica* means "opposite of Arctic." The Arctic is the area surrounding the North Pole.

Antarctica is the coldest and windiest place on Earth. The average temperature in Antarctica is –30 °F (–34.4 °C). The coldest temperature ever recorded was at the South Pole in 1983. The temperature that day was –128.6 °F (–89.2 °C).

98 percent of Antarctica is covered by this ice cap.

Ice Cap

A giant sheet of ice covers 98 percent of Antarctica. The other 2 percent is bare rock. These rocky areas are called *oases* and are found along the coast. Almost 70 percent of all the world's fresh water is located in the ice sheet. However, the continent gets no rain and very little snow. The average thickness of the ice cap is 1.5 miles. The ice is not solid everywhere, however. At the edges of Antarctica, giant glaciers and chunks of ice constantly break off and fall into the ocean. These pieces of ice become icebergs. The icebergs are dangerous to ships because they may be hidden beneath the surface. They can cause great damage if a ship hits one. The icebergs slowly melt as they float into warmer waters.

Plant and Animal Life

Antarctica is almost empty of plants and animals. The temperature is too cold to sustain most life. However, some mosses, plants, and flowers grow in areas near the coast. These areas are not covered with ice.

Over forty different types of birds make Antarctica their home. One type of bird is the penguin. Penguin varieties such as the emperor and chinstrap live on the coast and on some of the islands around Antarctica. They thrive in the cold climate. Seals and whales swim in the waters surrounding the ice cap. Cod and icefish can also be found swimming in the cold waters.

People

 People began exploring Antarctica in 1895. Two famous English explorers traveled to Antarctica between 1902 and 1915. Their names were Robert F. Scott and Henry Shackleton. They explored areas deep inside Antarctica. On December 14, 1911, Roald Amundsen became the first person to reach the South Pole.

Every year, hundreds of researchers and scientists travel to Antarctica to study the ice caps and climate. Scientists use tools to drill through the ice. By studying samples from the layers of ice, scientists learn more about climate change. Antarctica does not have any permanent residents. That is because it is almost impossible to live in Antarctica's freezing temperatures, strong winds, and blizzards.

HEADINGS Headings in a text tell the reader what each section of the text is about. How does the heading "Plant and Animal Life" at the top of this page help you understand what you are about to read?

ASK AND ANSWER QUESTIONS What is a question you could ask yourself when you read the heading "Plant and Animal Life"?

Comprehension Check

Look back at the sample Web page in "Using the Internet."
Using information from the Web page, write an effect next to each cause listed in the chart.

Causes		Effects
Antarctica has freezing temperatures, strong winds, and blizzards.	→	
Ice covers 98% of the land.	→	
Icebergs break off from the ice cap and enter the ocean.	→	
Scientists travel there to study the ice cap and the climate.	→	

Vocabulary

Use the word map below to help you define and use one of the highlighted vocabulary words from the Share and Learn reading or another word your teacher assigns you.

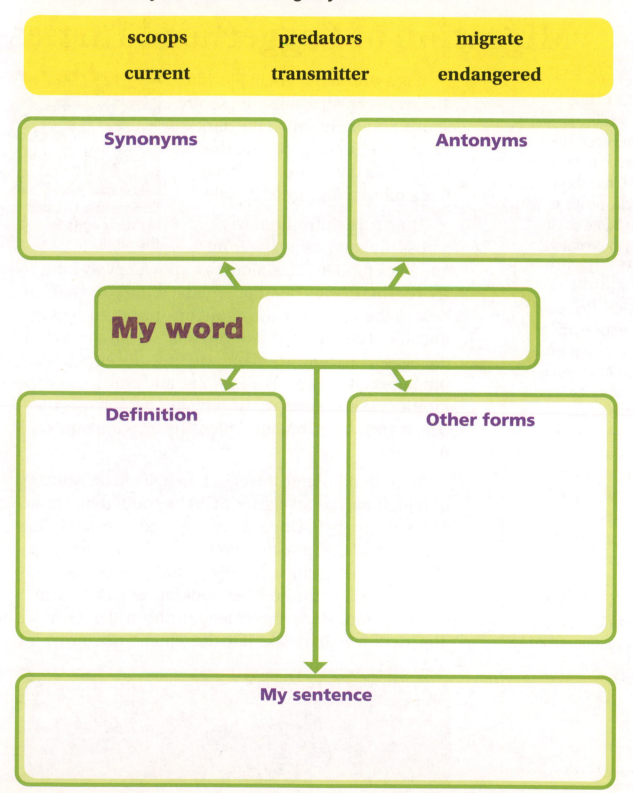

| scoops | predators | migrate |
| current | transmitter | endangered |

Synonyms

Antonyms

My word

Definition

Other forms

My sentence

Consider ▶ What are some different tools scientists use to study animals?

Why is it important to understand how we affect the world around us?

Migration of Loggerhead Turtles

1 It is a summer night in Florida. The waves crash against the sandy shore. Suddenly, out in the dark water, a large shape rises to the surface and swims to the beach. It is a mother loggerhead turtle.

Loggerhead turtles lay their eggs in the sand.

The turtle clumsily crawls across the sand using her front and back flippers. She chooses a spot far away from shore. Then, using her flippers, she scoops out a deep hole in the sand. She lays about one hundred eggs in the hole. The eggs look like golf balls. Next, she covers the eggs with sand. The sand will hide the eggs from predators such as birds, raccoons, and crabs. Once the mother covers the eggs, she wriggles back across the beach and slides into the water. The eggs are now on their own.

Two months later, the eggs hatch. Each baby turtle, or hatchling, has an egg tooth on its snout that it uses to break the shell. Once out of the shell, the hatchlings climb out of the nest and scramble toward the water. They need to be quick, however. Birds, raccoons, and crabs roam the beaches, looking for a chance to devour them. Many loggerhead turtles will not survive. The lucky few that make it to the water swim away.

CONTEXT CLUES
What words in paragraph 2 help you understand the meaning of the word scoops? Circle them. Then circle the words that help you figure out the meaning of predators.

SEQUENCE Underline the sequence words and phrases in paragraph 2 that describe how the loggerhead turtle lays her eggs in the sand.

ASK AND ANSWER QUESTIONS Look back at paragraph 3. What are some of the dangers hatchlings face after they are born? Write the answer below. Then underline text that answers your question.

_____

_____

_____

This hatchling heads for the safety of the ocean.

Many years later, the female turtles return to the same beach they left when they were hatchlings. The adult turtles <mark>migrate</mark> thousands of miles to lay their eggs on the same beaches where they were born.

5   Why do turtles migrate? How do they know where to go? Where do the female turtles go after they lay their eggs? For many years, the migration pattern of loggerhead turtles was a mystery. Then scientists developed different ways to track the migration of loggerhead turtles throughout their lives.

Where Do They Go?

Scientists have begun to understand more about how turtles migrate after they are born. Once the hatchlings reach the water, they swim away from the shore as quickly as possible. This helps them escape birds and fish hunting near the shore. The hatchlings swim for one to two days. They are then swept up into the Gulf Stream <mark>current</mark>. The current pushes the hatchlings north along the coast of the United States. The current is also filled with floating seaweed. The hatchlings spend many years feeding on and hiding in the seaweed until they become adults. By that point they are too big to be eaten by most predators.

CONTEXT CLUES
What words help you understand the meaning of the word <mark>migrate</mark>? Circle them.

HEADINGS Read the heading on this page. What do you think you will learn from reading this section?

_____

_____

_____

Scientists are not sure where hatchling loggerheads spend their early years.

USE MAPS Look at the map on this page. Describe the route loggerhead turtles take around the Atlantic Ocean.

_____

_____

_____

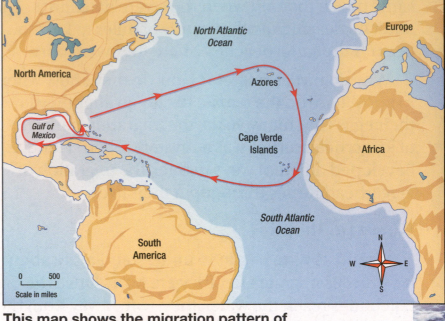

This map shows the migration pattern of loggerhead turtles.

CONTEXT CLUES Circle the words that help you figure out the meaning of transmitter in paragraph 9.

STEPS IN A PROCESS Paragraph 9 describes the process of tracking a turtle by satellite. What happens first in this process?

_____

_____

_____

For the next five to ten years, the turtles migrate across the Atlantic Ocean to Europe. They swim down toward the western edge of Africa. Finally, the current pushes the turtles back across the Atlantic. At the end of their journey, they have traveled 8,000 miles. They come back to where it all began.

A Game of Tag

Because they spend the majority of their time in water, loggerhead turtles are not easy to track. They also migrate thousands of miles to find food. Scientists have developed several ways to track these turtles.

One way is by using satellites. Scientists attach a high-tech tag to the shell of a mother turtle. This tag carries a radio transmitter. Whenever the turtle rises to the surface of the water to breathe, the transmitter beams a signal to a satellite orbiting Earth. The satellite then beams the information back to Earth. After a year, the transmitter stops working and falls off the turtle.

Satellites send information about loggerhead turtles to scientists on land.

CAUSE AND EFFECT
Reread paragraph 11. Why do you think scientists offer people a reward for returning the tags?

_____

_____

_____

ASK AND ANSWER QUESTIONS
Reread paragraph 12. Why do scientists take blood samples from loggerhead turtles?

_____

_____

_____

10   Scientists use a computer program to organize the information from the satellite and track the turtle. Scientists can see where the turtle is traveling. They can see how fast the turtle is swimming. Scientists can also find out where the turtle swims to feed.

Another tracking method is placing a tag on a turtle's flipper. Each tag has a number and a message. The message asks people to return the tag to the scientists for a small reward. Scientists use the tags to map where the turtles have been.

A third way scientists study the migration of loggerhead turtles is by taking blood samples. They compare the blood from one turtle with the blood of other turtles to find out whether any of the turtles are related. Because turtles return to the same beach to lay eggs, turtles that came from the same beach should have similar blood. The blood samples can tell scientists where turtles were born.

CAUSE AND EFFECT
What do you think might happen if people did not try to protect turtles?

_____

_____

_____

Many turtles are accidentally caught in fishing nets.

Turtle Safety

Loggerhead turtles are ==endangered==. This means there are not many of them left. Scientists know that understanding the turtles' migration patterns will help protect the turtles. If people know where the turtles like to swim, people can watch out for them. Boats can be careful not to collide with the turtles. Knowing where the turtles swim also tells scientists where turtles find their food. They can warn people fishing to be careful about where they cast their nets so they don't catch the turtles by accident. Governments can also ban fishing in the areas where turtles feed.

Scientists know more about turtles now than they ever did before. By using technology, they know that turtles migrate across the Atlantic before returning home to lay their eggs. By studying where the turtles migrate, we can help save them from going away forever.

Anchor Standard Discussion Questions

Discuss the following questions with your peer group. Then record your answers in the space provided.

1. What is the purpose of the first four paragraphs of "Migration of Loggerhead Turtles"? How are they different from the rest of the passage? Support your answers with details from the text.

_____

_____

_____

_____

_____

_____

2. Choose three images from "Migration of Loggerhead Turtles." How does each image deepen your understanding of the text? Support your answers with details from the text.

_____

_____

_____

_____

_____

_____

Comprehension Check

1. What are the three ways scientists track loggerhead turtles?

_____

_____

_____

2. How does our knowing where loggerhead turtles swim help us protect them?

_____

_____

_____

3. Which turtle-tracking method used by scientists do you think is the best one? Why?

_____

_____

_____

Read On Your Own

Read another technical text, "Swimming with Sharks," independently. Apply what you learned in this lesson and check your understanding.

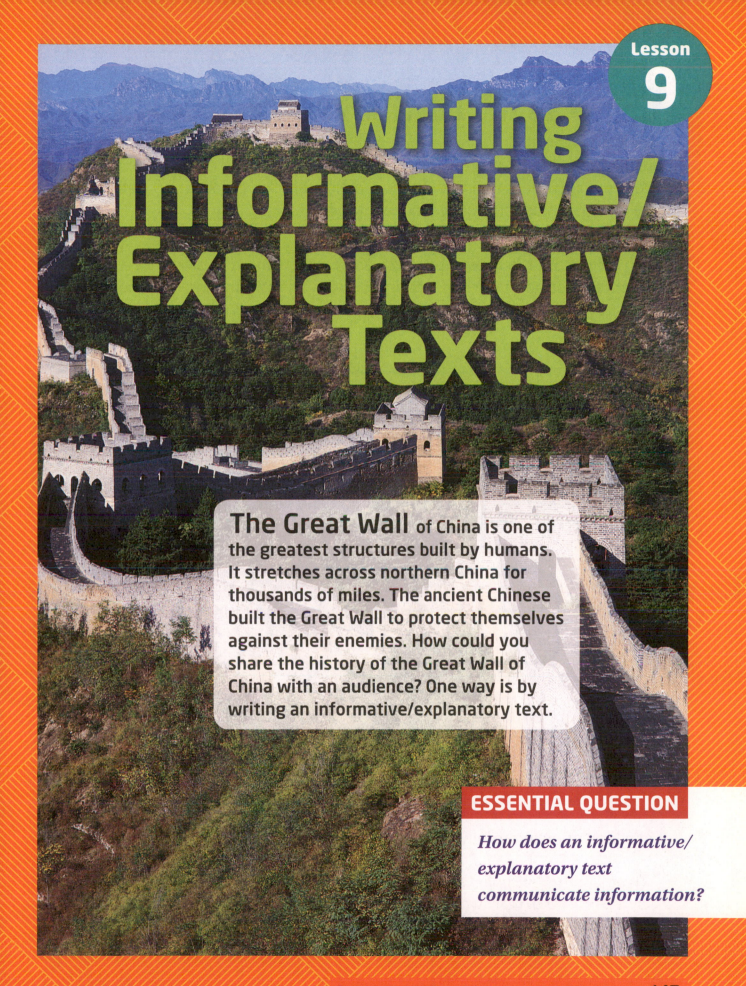

Writing Informative/ Explanatory Texts

The Great Wall of China is one of the greatest structures built by humans. It stretches across northern China for thousands of miles. The ancient Chinese built the Great Wall to protect themselves against their enemies. How could you share the history of the Great Wall of China with an audience? One way is by writing an informative/explanatory text.

ESSENTIAL QUESTION

How does an informative/ explanatory text communicate information?

What's an Informative/Explanatory Text?

The Great Wall of China has a long and interesting history. Workers began building the Great Wall in 220 BCE. It is made of brick, dirt, and stone. It took two thousand years to finish. These are all examples of facts and details that you can find in an informative/explanatory text.

In an **informative/explanatory text**, you present information about a specific subject and support it with facts and details. The information is presented in a clear way for the reader. Read the ways to make your informative/explanatory text effective.

Introduction
The introduction tells your reader what you are writing about. The introduction is interesting. It also grabs the reader's attention and states the topic.

Body
The body includes details that support the topic. It provides facts, details, and explanations.

Conclusion
The conclusion is satisfying and sums up your text in a memorable way.

Let's look at an informative/explanatory text.

Analyze a Mentor Text

This is an example of an informative/explanatory text by a third grader. Read it and then complete the activities in the boxes as a class.

Roman Arches

The ancient Romans are famous for their architecture. Architecture is the art and science of making buildings. Roman buildings were very sturdy because they were constructed using the simple shape of a curved arch. An arch is the shape of a half-circle. The Romans were among the first people to use arches in buildings.

Because arches were strong and attractive, they could be used to design graceful buildings. The Romans used cut stone and concrete to make their arches. They created a type of concrete that was very strong, and it dried quickly, too.

In addition, arches were very useful. In earlier times, most entrances to buildings were made of two posts with a large stone laid across the top. However, the stone cracked if it was too heavy. Arches were made with smaller and lighter stones that fit together. Furthermore, the curved shape of the arch spread the weight of the stones, so no part was too heavy. Therefore, the arch did not break.

TOPIC The writer gets the reader's attention in the introduction. The writer also states the topic, the Roman arch. Draw a box around the topic sentence.

SUPPORTING DETAILS The writer uses details in the second and third paragraphs that support the topic sentence. Underline the explanations, details, or facts in the paragraphs.

stone block

post

arch

By using the arch, Roman builders were able to construct larger and stronger buildings and structures.

The Romans used arches to build many buildings and structures. For example, theaters, baths, and bridges were built using the arch. One of the most important structures built with the arch was the aqueduct. Rows of arch after arch made the aqueducts look like big pieces of lace. Aqueducts were bridges that brought water into cities. They were many miles long, stretching from the mountains to the cities around the Roman Empire. Millions of people relied on the aqueducts to get their water.

The arch was very important to Roman architecture and was used in structures all across Rome. If you ever go to Rome, you can look for the arches in the ruins of ancient buildings. They give us a hint of how buildings were constructed long ago.

Think About It ▶ Why do you think the author chose to write about the Roman arch?

What did you learn about the Roman arch? Have you seen such arches anywhere else?

Vocabulary Study: Using Glossaries and Dictionaries

A **dictionary** is a book in which words are listed alphabetically with their meanings, pronunciations, and other information. A **glossary** is a list of hard words and their meanings that is usually printed at the end of a book. A dictionary is like a glossary, but a dictionary includes thousands of words used in the English language.

Read the following passage with the class or a partner.

> The **ruins** of the ancient city of Rome stretched for as far as the eye could see. On the hillside, the **remains** of a large temple sat under the hot sun. Visitors walked around the marble pillars and snapped pictures with their cameras.

The bold words would be defined in the book's glossary. You could also look them up in a dictionary. Look at the dictionary entries below.

> re • main /ri mān′/ 1. *verb* To stay in the same place 2. *noun* A part that is left over
>
> ru • in /ro͞o′ in/ 1. *noun* A building, city, or area that has been destroyed 2. *verb* To destroy or damage beyond repair

Work with your class or a partner to answer the questions below.

1. How many syllables are in the word *remain*? _____

2. Which definition of *ruin* is used in the passage? _____

3. How many definitions are given for the word *ruin*? _____

4. Is *ruin* used as a noun or a verb in the passage? _____

Writing Process

Now that you have read and analyzed an informative/explanatory text, you are going to create your own by following these steps of the writing process.

1. Get Ready: Take Notes on Research Research information from a text and take notes. Research visual information about a topic and take notes.

2. Organize Use a graphic organizer to organize and plan your informative/explanatory text.

3. Draft Create the first draft of your informative/explanatory text.

4. Peer Review Work with a partner to evaluate and improve your draft.

5. Revise Use suggestions from your peer review to revise your writing.

6. Edit Check your work carefully for spelling, punctuation, and grammar errors.

7. Publish Create a final version of your informative/explanatory text.

Writing Assignment

In this lesson, you will write your own informative/explanatory text. As you create this piece, remember the elements of the mentor text that were most effective. Read the following assignment.

> Research the Great Wall of China. Then write three to five paragraphs about the history of the Great Wall, including why it was built, how it was built, who built it, and what the Great Wall is like today.

1. Get Ready: Take Notes on Research

The writer of the mentor text wrote about Roman architecture and the arch. Before he could write a draft, he researched his topic. Here is a paragraph from one of the books he found.

> Roman architects had two advantages: the use of concrete, and the invention of the arch. Romans discovered that mixing volcanic ash with gravel and seawater made a strong concrete that was almost unbreakable. Concrete was also cheaper and stronger than stone and was perfect for constructing large buildings. The arch allowed Roman architects to build doorways with shaped stones that "arched" over two pillars. Arches used less stone and were stronger than regular doorways. The Romans used concrete and arches to build some of their most beautiful structures, including bridges, aqueducts, and domes.

The writer took notes on each of the books he found. Here is the note card that he filled out for the text above. What kinds of information does he include?

MAIN IDEA On the first line, he wrote the main idea from the passage that he wanted to use in his report.

Main Idea: Concrete and the arch gave Roman architects two advantages.

Detail: Arches used less stone and were stronger than regular doorways.

Detail: Romans used concrete and the arch to build bridges, aqueducts, and domes.

Source: *Roman Architecture* by Tracie Telling

DETAILS He next listed notes about details from the passage. How do the details support the main idea?

SOURCE Finally, he wrote where he had found the passage. Where did he find this passage?

Researching Text

Your topic is the Great Wall of China. Here is some information that you might use in your informative piece. Read the text. Think about the important ideas in each paragraph. Also think about interesting details that you might use in your informative piece.

MAIN IDEA What do you think is the main idea in the first paragraph?

DETAILS Which interesting explanations, details, or facts would you use in your informative/explanatory text?

DETAILS The second paragraph describes how soldiers guarded the wall. Which details do you find most interesting in the paragraph?

from *China's Great Wall*
by D. Everett Tunard

Construction on the Great Wall of China started over 2,000 years ago, around 221 BCE. The wall was built by soldiers, peasants, and criminals. Different materials were used to build the wall. Most of the materials used were found in the area. For example, in rocky areas the wall was made of stone. If stone could not be found, then pounded dirt was used. In later years, the wall was made of brick.

If the wall was attacked, the soldiers defending the wall used different ways to communicate with each other. Stone towers were built near the wall. These towers were built on high ground so they could be seen easily by soldiers in nearby towers. Once the enemy was spotted, soldiers built a fire on top of the platform of the tower. The soldiers guarding the next tower over saw the smoke and built their own fire on top of their own platform. Sometimes the soldiers fired cannons to warn the soldiers in other towers that the enemy was near.

Try It!   Record Your Notes

Use these note cards to take notes on the text about the Great Wall of China. Remember, write the main idea and interesting details of each paragraph. Finally, give the source of the information.

Main Idea:
Detail:
Detail:
Detail:
Source:

Main Idea:
Detail:
Detail:
Detail:
Source:

Researching Visual Information

When you research a topic, you will discover that information can be given in different ways. You may find photographs or diagrams in online resources. You may find information given in charts and tables. You can use note cards to record notes about these different forms of information, too.

The first example below shows a diagram of the Great Wall. The second example shows a map of the wall. Think about how you could use both to get ideas and details about the Great Wall of China.

INFORMATION FROM RESOURCES This diagram shows an inside view of how the wall was built. Labels point to parts of the wall and to the materials from which the wall was made. What do you learn about the wall from this diagram?

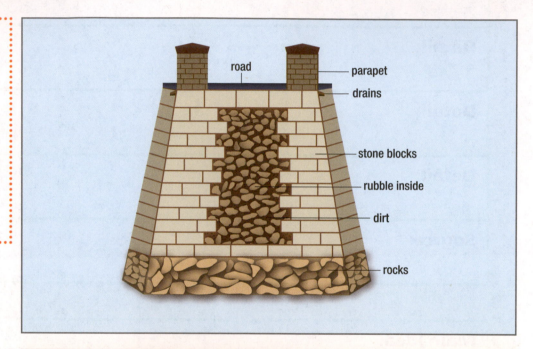

INFORMATION FROM RESOURCES How could this map help you write an informational text about where the Great Wall of China is located? What information would you use?

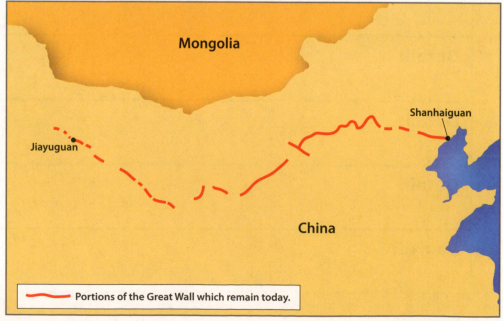

Try It!   Record Your Notes

Use these note cards to take notes on the diagram and map shown on the previous page. You can use your answers from the activities on that page to help you.

Main Idea (Diagram):

Detail:

Detail:

Detail:

Source:

Main Idea (Map):

Detail:

Detail:

Detail:

Source:

2. Organize

You are almost ready to begin a draft of your informative/explanatory text. You can use a graphic organizer to help organize the ideas and details. You can then refer to the graphic organizer as you work through the different parts of your draft. The writer of the mentor text completed this graphic organizer.

INTRODUCTION In the first paragraph, you tell the topic of your informative/ explanatory text.

SUPPORTING PARAGRAPHS In the second, third, and fourth paragraphs, you elaborate on the topic with explanations, details, and facts that support the topic.

Later you will be including at least three supporting details in your draft.

CONCLUSION Your last paragraph should include a satisfying conclusion that briefly sums up the text.

Main Idea
Roman buildings were very sturdy because they were constructed using the simple shape of a curved arch.

Supporting Detail 1
Arches were made of cut stone and concrete. The Romans used concrete that was very strong and dried quickly.

Supporting Detail 2
Arches were made with smaller and lighter stones that fit together. The weight of the arch was spread out.

Supporting Detail 3
Romans built lots of things using arches. Arches were used in theaters, baths, bridges, and aqueducts.

Conclusion
The arch was very important to Roman architecture. They were made of concrete and used in buildings all across Rome.

Try It!

Organize Your Informative/Explanatory Text

Now use the graphic organizer below to organize the ideas and details you want to use in the different paragraphs of your draft.

Main Idea

Supporting Detail 1

Supporting Detail 2

Supporting Detail 3

Conclusion

3. Draft

Now it is time to write the first draft of your informative/explanatory text. Remember, your draft does not have to be perfect! This is the time to use your notes, get your ideas down in some sort of organized way, and have fun. You will have time to revise your writing later. Start by drafting your informative/explanatory text on a computer or on a separate sheet of paper. Tell about the Great Wall of China.

Writer's Craft: Using Linking Words and Phrases to Connect Ideas

Linking words and phrases help writing flow smoothly. They also help readers understand how ideas are connected. Here are some common linking words and phrases.

Linking words	after, also, although, another, and, because, but, furthermore, however, therefore
Linking phrases	as well, even though, as long as, in addition, in contrast

The author of the mentor text uses linking words and phrases in his third paragraph.

LINKING WORDS AND PHRASES
Read this section of the mentor text. Circle the linking words and phrases that connect ideas.

In addition, arches were very useful. In earlier times, most entrances to buildings were made of two posts with a large stone laid across the top. However, the stone cracked if it was too heavy. Arches were made with smaller and lighter stones that fit together. Furthermore, the curved shape of the arch spread the weight of the stones, so no part was too heavy. Therefore, the arch did not break.

Try It!   Write Your First Draft

On a computer or a separate sheet of paper, create the draft of your informative/explanatory text. Remember to use linking words and phrases in your writing. Use this drafting checklist to help you as you write.

✔ A good beginning gets your reader's attention. You can begin with a question or an interesting fact about your topic.

✔ Be sure to state your main idea in the first paragraph.

✔ Be sure every paragraph includes details that support the main idea.

✔ In each supporting paragraph, include sentences with explanations, details, and facts.

✔ Elaborate your text with visuals, such as photographs or graphics.

✔ Write a conclusion that is satisfying and sums up your text in a memorable way.

Tips for Writing Your First Draft

- Write down key phrases and ideas before you begin writing. Sometimes this is a great warm-up to get you started!

- Focus on ideas, not details. Since you will revise and edit later, you can fix the details then. In drafting, it's the ideas that count.

- Make sure all of your ideas are connected. Use the linking words and phrases listed on page 160 to help you connect ideas within your paragraphs.

4. Peer Review

After you finish your draft, you can work with a partner to review each other's drafts. Here is a draft of the mentor text. Read it with your partner. Together, answer the questions in the boxes. Then we'll see how the writer's classmate evaluated the draft.

An Early Draft:

Roman Arches

Romans are famous. They are famous for their architecture. What made it strong was the simple shape of a curved arch. The Romans were the first people to use arches in buildings. Rome also had forums. These were large squares where people gathered to talk.

Romans used cut stone and concrete to make their arches. Many buildings were made of marble. There are many marble buildings in Greece.

Arches were very useful. Before, most entrances to buildings were made of two posts with a stone laid across the top. The stone cracked if it was too heavy. Arches were made with smaller and lighter stones that fit together. The curved shape of the arch spread the weight of the stones so one part was not too heavy. Therefore, the arch did not break.

Romans built lots of things using arches. Arches were used in many buildings. In addition, arches were used in aqueducts. They were many miles long. People needed the aqueducts to get water.

The arch was very important to Roman architecture. You should go to Italy. There you can see Roman ruins. Ruins give an idea of what life was like during Roman times. You can walk around them and think about what the buildings looked like thousands of years ago.

INTRODUCTION In his draft, the writer does not have a clear main idea. Is the text about the arch or forums?

SUPPORTING PARAGRAPHS The second paragraph talks about marble. These details do not support the main idea. What changes would you make to this paragraph?

CONCLUSION The conclusion does not really sum up the text. How would you sum up the text?

An Example Peer Review Form

This peer review form gives an example of how a classmate evaluated the draft of the mentor text shown on the last page.

The introduction states the topic in an interesting way. **The main idea of the text is clear.**	You did a good job of *getting the reader's attention.* You could improve your informative/explanatory text by *writing a clearer main idea. Your main idea was confusing.*
The writer supports the main idea with at least three strong supporting details. **The writer includes explanations, details, and facts.**	You did a good job of *giving three supporting details.* You could improve your informative/explanatory text by *adding more explanations, details, or facts to the fourth paragraph.*
The writer uses linking words and phrases to make the writing flow smoothly.	You did a good job of *using "therefore" in the third paragraph.* You could improve your informative/explanatory text by *adding linking words and phrases such as "before," "however," and "furthermore."*
The writer includes a satisfying conclusion. **The conclusion sums up the text.**	You did a good job of *including a concluding statement.* You could improve your informative/explanatory text by *adding one or two sentences that briefly summarize your topic.*

Try It!   Peer Review with a Partner

Now you are going to work with a partner to review each other's informative/explanatory text drafts. You will use the peer review form below. If you need help, look back at the mentor text writer's peer review form for suggestions.

The introduction states the topic in an interesting way. **The main idea of the text is clear.**	You did a good job of --- You could improve your informative/explanatory text by
The writer supports the main idea with at least three strong supporting details. **The writer includes explanations, details, and facts.**	You did a good job of --- You could improve your informative/explanatory text by
The writer uses linking words and phrases to make the writing flow smoothly.	You did a good job of --- You could improve your informative/explanatory text by
The writer includes a satisfying conclusion. **The conclusion sums up the text.**	You did a good job of --- You could improve your informative/explanatory text by

Try It!

Record Key Peer Review Comments

Now it's time for you and your partner to share your comments with each other. Listen to your partner's feedback, and write down the key comments in the left column. Then write some ideas for improving your draft in the right column.

My review says that my introduction	I will
My review says that my main idea	I will
My review says that my use of supporting details	I will
My review says that my use of linking words	I will
My review says that my conclusion	I will

Use the space below to write anything else you notice about your draft that you think you can improve.

5. Revise

In this step of the writing process, you will work on parts of your draft that need improvement. Use the peer review form that your classmate completed to help you. Also use your own ideas about how to improve each part of your informative/explanatory text. This checklist includes some things to think about as you get ready to revise.

Revision Checklist

✓ Does my beginning catch the reader's interest? Do I state my main idea clearly?

✓ Do all of my explanations, details, and facts support the main idea?

✓ Is my conclusion interesting? Have I summed up the text well?

✓ Do I use linking words and phrases to connect ideas?

✓ Do I use precise language to make my ideas as clear as can be?

Writer's Craft: Using Literal and Nonliteral Language

Sometimes writers use both literal and nonliteral language to add flavor to their writing. For example, they might write, "Paula sings like a bird." The writer is comparing Paula's singing voice with a bird's lovely song. Now look at the mentor text for examples of nonliteral language.

LITERAL AND NONLITERAL LANGUAGE Writers use nonliteral language such as figures of speech in their writing. Underline the figure of speech in this paragraph.

The Romans used arches to build many buildings and structures. For example, theaters, baths, and bridges were built using the arch. One of the most important structures built with the arch was the aqueduct. Rows of arch after arch made the aqueducts look like big pieces of lace.

Try It!

Revise Your Informative/Explanatory Text

Replacing simple words with more descriptive or precise words is an important part of revising. Practice using precise language with the following paragraph. Replace each underlined word with a more precise, interesting word. Write your answers on the lines below the paragraph.

In 312 BCE, the Roman began to <u>make</u> bridges to bring water into Rome. These bridges were called aqueducts. The aqueducts were <u>big</u>. The water inside moved very <u>fast</u>. The water came from the mountains, so it must have been <u>cold</u>!

Replace *make* with _____

Replace *big* with _____

Replace *fast* with _____

Replace *cold* with _____

Writing Assignment

Now it's time to revise the draft of your informative/explanatory text. Continue working on a computer or on a separate sheet of paper. Review the assignment, repeated below, and the checklist. Doing so will help you know that you have included everything you need.

Writing Assignment

Research the Great Wall of China. Then write three to five paragraphs about the history of the Great Wall, including why it was built, how it was built, who built it, and what the Great Wall is like today.

6. Edit

After revising your informative/explanatory text, you will edit it. When you edit, you read very carefully to be sure to find any mistakes in your writing. Here's a checklist of some things to look for as you edit.

Editing Checklist

✓ Did you indent each paragraph?

✓ Are all of your sentences complete? Does each have a subject and a verb?

✓ Did you begin each sentence with a capital letter?

✓ Does each sentence end with the correct punctuation?

✓ Have you used commas correctly?

✓ Are all of your words spelled correctly?

You can use these editing marks to mark any errors you find.

⌄ Add   ⌎ Delete   / Change capital letter to lowercase
⊙ Insert period

This paragraph from an early draft of the mentor text shows how to use editing marks.

The Romans built lots of things using arches.

Arches were used in Theaters Baths, and Bridges.

In addition arches were used in aqueducts.

Aqueducts were bridges that brought ~~into~~ water into

cities. They were many *miles* long. Millions of Romans

needed the aqueducts to get water⊙

Language Focus: Sentence Structure

A **simple sentence** has a subject and a predicate. A sentence begins with a capital letter and ends with a punctuation mark.

Example: Erica walked to the store.

A **compound sentence** contains two or more simple sentences, which are called main clauses. To connect the main clauses in a compound sentence, use a comma plus a **coordinating conjunction**. *And*, *but*, *for*, *nor*, *so*, *yet*, and *or* are coordinating conjunctions.

Example: Erica walked to the store, but she didn't buy anything.

A **complex sentence** includes a main clause and one or more subordinate clauses. A subordinate clause has a subject and a predicate but does not stand alone as a sentence. A **subordinating conjunction** introduces a subordinate clause. *Although*, *after*, *as*, *because*, *before*, *until*, and *when* are some subordinating conjunctions.

Example: Before she walked to the store, Erica took a nap.

Because arches were strong and attractive, they could be used to design graceful buildings. The Romans used cut stone and concrete to make their arches. They created a type of concrete that was very strong, and it dried quickly, too.

SENTENCE STRUCTURE
Read this section of the mentor text. Use the information on this page to underline the simple sentence. Then circle the compound sentence and underline the comma and conjunction. Finally, draw a square around the complex sentence and underline the subordinate clause.

Try It! Language and Editing Practice

Rewrite each pair of sentences as one compound sentence. Use the coordinating conjunctions *or*, *so*, and *but*.

1. Jamie likes to read adventure stories. Gwen prefers mysteries.

   _____

2. Alaska is very cold in the winter. People must wear hats and scarves.

   _____

   _____

3. Do you want to go to the park? Do you want to watch a movie?

   _____

Read the following complex sentences. Underline the main clause once. Underline the subordinate clause twice.

4. Although he was scared of the water, Ricky climbed into the boat.

5. Alex needed to buy a present before the day was over.

Now use editing marks to correct the errors in this paragraph.

   During the third century BCE, Roman builders used Wood and Bricks made of mud? Later, the Romans began using concrete. When it dried concrete was as hard as stone. Because concrete was weatherproof it was perfect for building bridge

Try It!   Edit Your Informative/Explanatory Text

Now edit your informative/explanatory text. Use this checklist and the editing marks you have learned to correct any errors you find.

- [ ] Are all of your sentences complete?

- [ ] Are there any missing or repeated words in your sentences?

- [ ] Did you begin each sentence with a capital letter?

- [ ] Have you followed the rules of capitalization?

- [ ] Have you used the correct conjunction in your compound sentences?

Editing Tips

- Use your finger or a pencil to point at each word as you read it. This will help you slow down and find easy-to-miss mistakes.

- Listen carefully as you read. Do you need to take a breath when you're reading some of the sentences? That usually indicates sentences that need punctuation.

- Read your writing over at a slow pace at least two times. When reading for small details, one reading is not enough!

7. Publish

On a computer or a separate sheet of paper, create a neat final draft of your informative/explanatory text. Correct all errors that you identified while editing your draft. Be sure to give your informative/explanatory text an interesting title.

The final step is to publish your informative/explanatory text. Here are some different ways you might choose to share your work.

- Read aloud your informative/explanatory text to your class or to a small group of your classmates.

- Create an old-fashioned newspaper that describes the Great Wall of China.

- Create a travel book about the Great Wall of China.

- Create a poster using your informative/explanatory text and drawings or photographs from magazines or newspapers.

Technology Suggestions

- **Publish your informative/explanatory text in a multimedia presentation using digital images and photographs.**
- **Create a simple Web page about the Great Wall of China.**

Reading Scientific Nonfiction

Look at this picture of students doing research.

What are some ways people learn about science?

ESSENTIAL QUESTION

What can we learn from articles about weather, animals, plants, and other science topics?

Consider ▶ Why do you think snow can be both fun and dangerous?

How do you find out when a storm is coming?

SCIENTIFIC NONFICTION

Scientific nonfiction provides true information about an area of science. An article might be in a magazine or newspaper, a textbook, an encyclopedia, or on a Web site. These articles usually include photos, diagrams, maps, graphs, and headings to help explain a topic. People read scientific nonfiction for research. Why else might people read scientific nonfiction?

CONTEXT CLUES

Sometimes when you're reading, you see a word you don't know. Context clues are nearby words that give clues to the unfamiliar word's meaning. Look at the word *blizzard* in paragraph 1. In paragraph 2, several words and phrases, including "winter storms," "bitterly cold," and "thick snow," tell you that a blizzard is a big, dangerous snowstorm. Look at the word *vapor* in paragraph 3. What context clues help you figure out its meaning? What does it mean?

Howling Wind, Swirling Snow

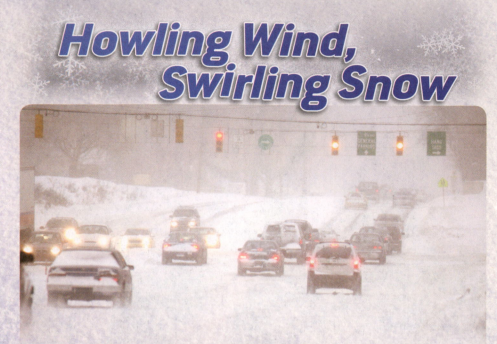

1 Every winter, children from Maine to Montana go to bed wishing for the next day to be a snow day. On snow days, school is closed because school buses and cars can't travel easily on snow-covered roads. Some children have heard the superstitions that they can make it snow by wearing their pajamas inside out or by sleeping with spoons under their pillows. They hope that in the morning, they will wake up and see huge piles of fluffy flakes outside their homes. If they knew a blizzard was coming, however, they might change their wish.

Snow days can be a lot of fun, but blizzards are not fun at all. These winter storms are extremely dangerous. The temperature is bitterly cold. Thick snow swirls until people can barely see in front of them. The wind can blow people right off their feet.

Buildings creak and trees sway. The storms go on and on. It becomes impossible for people to leave their homes to go anywhere.

How a Blizzard Starts

These fierce storms start like any snowfall. Snow is a form of water that falls to the ground, like rain, sleet, and hail. How does snow form? First, sunshine causes oceans and lakes to heat up. Then, as water evaporates, or changes into vapor, it rises into the air to form clouds. Next, the water vapor in the clouds freezes and forms ice. Tiny bits of ice grow into snowflakes. They get heavier and heavier. Finally, because they get so heavy, they fall to the ground. Cold winter air keeps them frozen as they fall.

A blizzard is not just any strong snowstorm. In a blizzard, there is so much snow falling or blowing that you can't see farther than a quarter of a mile in any direction. During a blizzard, this condition lasts at least three hours. Snow is just one part of a blizzard. Blizzards also have freezing temperatures and high-speed winds. The winds blow hard and fast, at least 35 miles per hour, and often more.

SEQUENCE The order in which events occur is called sequence. In paragraph 3, the word *first* tells you that the first step in forming snow is that the sunshine causes oceans and lakes to heat up. What words in the paragraph tell you the order of the other steps?

ASK AND ANSWER QUESTIONS You can better understand what you're reading by asking yourself questions and then reading on to find the answers. You might wonder what keeps snowflakes from melting as they fall and then read on to see that cold winter air keeps them frozen. What other question might you ask about a blizzard?

CAUSE AND EFFECT Cause and effect is the connection between events in which one event makes another happen. The cause is the event that makes something happen. The effect is the result of the cause. In paragraph 3, one cause is that snowflakes in the clouds get heavy. The effect is that the snowflakes fall to the ground. What is another cause and effect in this paragraph?

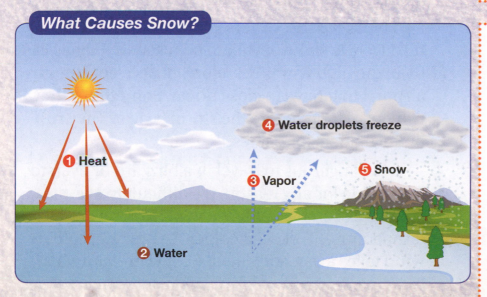

What Causes Snow?

1 Heat
2 Water
3 Vapor
4 Water droplets freeze
5 Snow

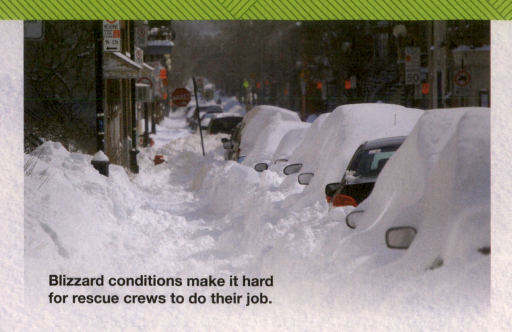

Blizzard conditions make it hard for rescue crews to do their job.

HEADINGS Look at the headings above the different sections of text. Headings can help you find information quickly and easily within the text. The heading "Not All Fun" lets you know that the text below it will be about the dangers of a blizzard. Under which heading would you look to find out how to get ready for a blizzard?

MAIN IDEA AND DETAILS The main idea of a paragraph tells what the paragraph is mostly about. It often comes at the start of a paragraph. Details are pieces of information that tell more about the main idea. In paragraph 5, the main idea is "Blizzards can cause serious damage." What details tell more about the kind of damage blizzards can cause?

CAUSE AND EFFECT In paragraph 6, one cause is heavy snowfall. One effect of that cause is that drivers cannot see. What other causes and effects do you see in that paragraph? What words in the paragraph show cause and effect?

Not All Fun

5   Blizzards can be exciting, but they're not all fun. Blizzards can cause serious damage. The strong winds and heavy snow can break tree branches or even knock whole trees down. Falling branches can snap power lines. Without power, most buildings don't have heat or light. Water pipes can freeze, so there's no running water. People shiver in the dark.

    A blizzard slows down transportation, too. Because the snowfall is so thick and white, it is nearly impossible for drivers to see. The heavy snow also blocks roads, so cars get stranded. Drivers hike through the snow or wait to be rescued. Planes can't fly in the high wind. Therefore, people get stuck in airports that have to close down. Sometimes they run out of food before the storm is over. They run out of diapers for babies.

    It is dangerous to travel in a blizzard or even to be outside for any reason. It's difficult to see, and it's also extremely cold. The wind can make freezing temperatures feel even colder. The strong, cold wind takes away body heat. People and animals can't live long in a blizzard because of the freezing cold wind.

People can't get to work, school, or the store during a blizzard. When the storm is over, it can take many hours—sometimes many days—to clear the snow and get everything repaired and back to normal.

Be Prepared

You can't stop a blizzard, but you can prepare for it. First, watch the weather report. Scientists who study weather, called meteorologists, use a lot of different tools to track storms. They also measure things such as a storm's wind speed. Weather satellites in space take pictures. The pictures from the satellites show where storms are starting, where they're heading, and how fast they're moving. If meteorologists know a storm is coming, they warn the public so people have time to make preparations.

10   If you hear a winter storm warning, then it's time to get busy. Stock up on food. Make sure any family members who need medicine have it. Have a good supply of water in bottles. Keep warm blankets and flashlights with extra batteries in the house and car. Most important, once the storm hits, stay inside. In a blizzard it is very easy to get lost because you can't see where you're going. If you have to go outside, wear layers of clothing to keep warm. Then tie a long rope to the door of the house and hold onto that rope the whole time you're outside so you will be able to find your way back.

And don't worry. Once the blizzard is over, there will still be plenty of snow around to make a snowman and have a fun snow day!

> **CONTEXT CLUES** In paragraph 9, use context clues to find out what the word *meteorologist* means.

> **PHOTOS WITH CAPTIONS** Photos can help you understand something you have read in text by giving you a visual image of it. A caption tells the main idea of the photo. What new information about meteorologists do you learn from the photo and caption on this page?

Meteorologists use data on computers to track storms.

Comprehension Check

Think about what you learned by reading "Howling Wind, Swirling Snow." Read the chart below. Go back to the article to find the information to fill in the missing cause or effect.

Cause	Effect
	There is no power to homes.
	Drivers cannot see.
Meteorologists tell people when a storm is coming.	

Vocabulary

Use the word map below to help you define and use one of the highlighted vocabulary words from the Share and Learn reading or another word your teacher assigns you.

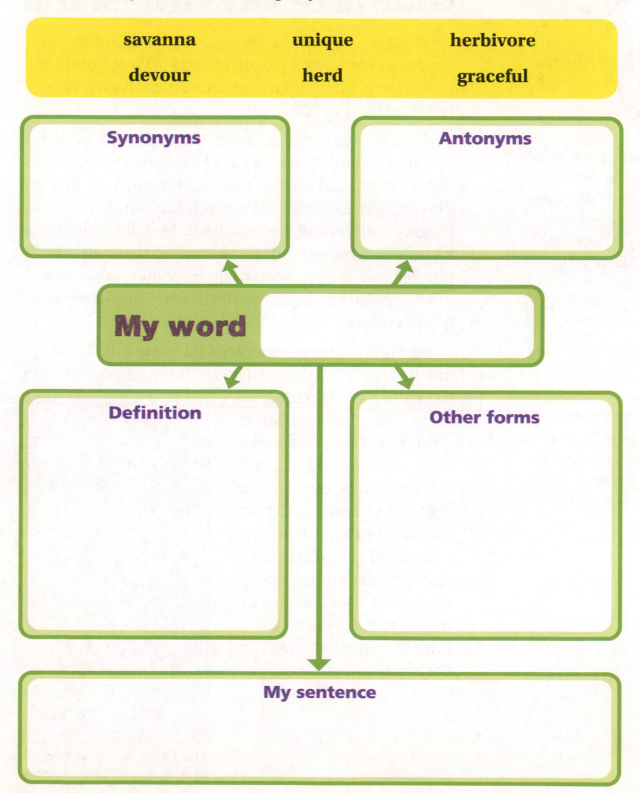

| savanna | unique | herbivore |
| devour | herd | graceful |

Synonyms

Antonyms

My word

Definition

Other forms

My sentence

Consider ▶ What makes giraffes different from other animals?

What helps giraffes survive in the place where they live?

Giants of the Grassland

1 What is as tall as the second story of a house, weighs as much as a pickup truck, and has a tongue that is longer than your foot-long ruler? It's a giraffe, the tallest animal on land!

Giraffes live in the <mark>savanna</mark>, or grasslands, of Africa. You might think that an animal that towers over all the others would be easy to spot, but you'd be wrong. The pattern on the giraffe's coat helps it hide in the bushes and trees of the grassland. And don't think that if you've seen one giraffe, you've seen them all. Each giraffe has a <mark>unique</mark> pattern on its coat—no two are alike. A baby giraffe can tell its mother just by looking at her pattern.

The giraffe has another special feature, its heart. The heart of any mammal has to pump blood through its body. A giraffe can grow up to 18 feet tall and weigh close to 1,800 pounds. Its legs can be 6 feet long, and its neck can be even longer. A giraffe's heart has to pump blood a long way to get it up to its head. You might think that a giraffe's heart would have to be supersized, like its body, but it's not. It's just built to pump very hard and very fast.

CONTEXT CLUES Which words in the second paragraph on this page give you a clue to the meaning of the word <mark>unique</mark>? Circle them.

MAPS Look at the map on this page. Draw an outline around the area where giraffes might live.

The beige areas on this map of Africa are the savanna.

Acacia tree

Acacia leaves are a favorite food of giraffes.

Feeding Time

Why would it help an animal to be so tall? A giraffe's size helps it survive in its environment. Giraffes are plant eaters, or herbivores. The savanna can be dry for long periods of time. It's difficult for many plants and trees to grow there. Most other savanna plant eaters, like zebras and antelopes, graze on grasses and shrubs that grow close to the ground. The giraffes get the leafy treetops almost all to themselves.

5 A giraffe's long tongue helps it grab leaves off tree branches. The tongue can be 18 inches long and can reach around thorns. The roof of a giraffe's mouth has grooves that help it strip leaves from branches. The giraffe reaches its long tongue around a branch, and as it pulls its head away, the leaves are stripped off the branch.

Giraffes need all the leaves they can get. Because they are such large animals, they have to eat a large amount of food. A giraffe can devour 75 pounds of leaves in just one day! But they only get a few leaves in each bite, so they may have to spend up to twenty hours a day eating to get enough.

PICTURE LABELS Labels are words or phrases that name something shown in a photograph or an illustration. In the photograph on this page, the label tells you what kind of tree the giraffe is eating from. What kind of tree is it?

MAIN IDEA AND DETAILS Which sentence tells you the main idea of paragraph 5? Underline it. Then list two details that support the main idea.

CAUSE AND EFFECT Reread paragraph 6. Why do giraffes spend a lot of time eating?

ASK AND ANSWER QUESTIONS One question you might ask yourself is, "How do giraffes warn each other about danger?" Draw a box around the part of the text that answers your question.

CONTEXT CLUES What does the word herd mean? Circle the context clues that help you decide.

_____

_____

_____

Getting Water

Leaves from trees supply giraffes not only with food but also with water. This source of water is important for two reasons. The first is that the savanna is very dry. If giraffes had to get all their water from ponds, lakes, streams, or rivers, they wouldn't survive.

The second reason is that drinking water at ground level is dangerous for giraffes. If a giraffe wants to drink from a stream or a lake, it has to spread its front legs far apart and bend its long neck all the way down to the water's surface. When the giraffe is bent over in this way, it's easier for a predator such as a lion or a crocodile to grab hold of it. When groups of giraffes do drink from a pond or lake, they take turns looking for predators. The giraffes will snort loudly to warn one another of danger.

Living Together

Giraffes travel together in large herds. The herds are made up of both male and female giraffes of all ages. Female giraffes carefully guard their babies during the first weeks of life. Baby giraffes cannot defend themselves. They depend on the other giraffes to protect them from predators. While mothers eat, the young giraffes stay in small nursery groups.

While one giraffe drinks, the others keep a lookout for predators.

Lions cannot run as fast as most of the animals they hunt. They must sneak up on their prey.

Staying Safe from Predators

10   Giraffes have very few predators. Lions and crocodiles are the only animals that hunt them. Being tall helps giraffes stay safe. A giraffe's long neck is like a lookout tower.

If a lion sees a giraffe grazing on treetops, it might try a sneak attack. The lion creeps closer and closer, trying not to make a sound. This method works well with other animals the lion hunts, such as water buffalo. But a giraffe almost always sees the lion coming.

Giraffes have help spotting predators, too. Tickbirds are little birds that ride on a giraffe's back. They eat insects off the giraffe's skin. When the tickbirds chirp loudly, the giraffe knows to look out.

If a giraffe spots a lion trying to sneak up on it or gets a warning from the tickbirds, the giraffe takes off running. Giraffes are surprisingly ==graceful== runners. They seem to float across the savanna. Their long legs help them run as fast as 35 miles an hour. That's about as fast as a car driving on a city street.

If a lion does catch up to a giraffe, the lion had better look out. A giraffe's legs aren't just good for running. They can kick really hard, too. A giraffe can kill a lion with just one kick.

SEQUENCE Reread the text on this page. List the sequence of events when a lion tries to sneak up on a giraffe. Use words like *next, then, after that,* and *last.*

First: lion sneaks up

_____

_____

_____

HEADINGS Read all the headings in the article. If you were looking for information on giraffes' eating habits, which section would you read? If you wanted to find out what animals eat giraffes, which section would you read? Underline the headings of the two sections you would read.

15 Being tall isn't always so great, though. Giraffes can't just flop down when they get tired. It's hard for them to get down because they're so big. It's also hard for them to get back up! Giraffes usually sleep standing up, but they occasionally sit or lie down when there are no predators around. Luckily, giraffes don't need much sleep. They sleep, on average, less than two hours every day.

Staying Strong

Many savanna animals, like elephants and rhinos, are endangered. They have lost places to live due to the destruction of their environment. They are also hunted and killed. There are so few of them left that they're in danger of disappearing from Earth forever. Fortunately, most giraffes are not endangered. There are fewer giraffes than there were a hundred years ago, but a large number still survive today. Only the Uganda giraffe is considered endangered. There are fewer than 500 of them in the wild.

Giraffes are in danger of losing their homes, though. When people need land to farm or build homes, giraffes can be in the way. People called giraffe wranglers help move giraffes to safe places. However, as more land is used for farming and homes, there will be fewer safe places left for giraffes.

The giraffes' great height and natural beauty make them stand out among the animals on the savanna. Hopefully, we will find these gentle giants there for a long, long time.

CONTEXT CLUES
Underline the sentence that tells you the meaning of the word *endangered*.

CAUSE AND EFFECT
Giraffes are in danger of losing their homes. Circle the words in the text that tell why.

Animals of all types gather at a watering hole.

Anchor Standard Discussion Question

Discuss the following question with your peer group. Then record your answer in the space provided.

1. "Giants of the Grassland" is a piece of scientific nonfiction that includes many facts about giraffes. But if you it read closely, you can learn something about the author, too. What is the author's opinion of giraffes? Do you think the author has a similar opinion about other savanna animals? Support your answers with details from the text.

_____

_____

_____

_____

_____

_____

_____

_____

_____

_____

_____

_____

_____

_____

Comprehension Check

1. How does a giraffe's size help it survive?

_____

_____

_____

2. Why do giraffes take turns when they drink at a lake or pond?

_____

_____

_____

3. How do giraffes protect themselves from predators?

_____

_____

_____

_____

Read On Your Own

Read another scientific nonfiction text, "Plants That Fight Back!", independently. Apply what you learned in this lesson and check your understanding.

Writing Opinion Pieces

Decisions can be hard. Groups often vote when they have to make decisions about important issues. Think about a decision that needs to be made with a vote because it affects a group. Before the voting takes place, you could try to convince other members of the group to agree with the choice you think is best. You could talk to people one by one to try to convince them to vote with you. Another way you could try to persuade them is by writing an opinion piece.

ESSENTIAL QUESTION

What makes an opinion piece effective?

What's an Opinion Piece?

Many families assign chores to each family member. One person might take out the garbage. Another might rake leaves or shovel snow. Maybe you think that your chores should change. You might think one family member should do more, and another should do less. Maybe you think that you shouldn't have to do any chores at all. Or maybe you'd like to do more challenging and interesting chores. These are all opinions.

In an **opinion piece**, you tell about your opinion and try to convince others to agree with you. Read the ways to make your opinion piece express your ideas strongly.

Your Opinion
State your opinion clearly. It should tell your readers exactly what you think or how you feel about a topic.

Supporting Reasons
Include at least three reasons to support your opinion. Supporting reasons should include facts, not just additional opinions. Strong supporting reasons will make your opinion piece more convincing.

Conclusion
Your conclusion sums up your ideas and completes your opinion piece.

Let's look at an effective opinion piece.

Analyze a Mentor Text

This is an example of an effective opinion piece by a third grader. Read it and then complete the activities in the boxes as a class.

Our Field Trip

The museum would be a better field trip than the zoo. At the zoo, the bears might be hiding in caves. The seals might be under the water. At the museum, we can see many more animals in less time. We should visit the natural history museum.

At the museum, the coolest animals are all clearly placed in glass showcases and can be seen most easily. We won't have to waste the class's valuable time looking for animals that aren't even out where we can see them. Also, we can read the most interesting facts about each animal in the showcases. The bigger animals' habitats are painted, which shows their natural environment. We can learn about these animals faster than we could at the zoo.

At both the museum and the zoo, we can learn about animals from faraway places. However, only at the museum can we see animals that have been extinct for thousands or millions of years. For example, we might see dinosaur skeletons. We also might see exhibits on woolly mammoths or saber-toothed tigers. Therefore, we can learn how the natural world has changed over time.

OPINION The writer gets the reader's attention in the introduction. Then the writer states an opinion about the field trip. Draw a box around the opinion.

SUPPORTING REASONS In the second and third paragraphs, the writer gives reasons that support the opinion. Underline the reasons in each paragraph.

SUPPORTING REASONS In the fourth paragraph, the writer gives another reason to support the opinion. Underline the reason in the paragraph.

CONCLUSION The writer sums up the supporting reasons in the conclusion. Underline the sentence that sums up the supporting reasons.

Another reason to visit the museum is that we can plan the field trip for any time. We could go there when we have been learning about some of the animals on display. We don't need to wait until the weather is nice in the spring. We won't have to risk postponing the trip because of rain.

In conclusion, if we are going to spend the day away from school, we need to use this time wisely. We can't take field trips every week. We need to get as much out of each trip as we can. We can definitely learn much more in one day at the museum than we could hope to at the zoo. That is why I know we must visit the natural history museum.

Think About It ▶ Whom do you think the writer is trying to convince with this opinion piece?

Do you think the reader is likely to be persuaded by the opinion piece? Why or why not?

Vocabulary Study: Identify Real-life Connections

Words can indicate or connect to a person's state of mind and opinions. The writer of the mentor text says the class can "definitely" learn more at the museum than at the zoo. The word *definitely* tells you the writer's opinion is very certain. The word *possibly* would indicate a less strong opinion.

In your writing, you can express your opinions using words with varying shades of meaning. If you feel strongly about a point, you can use words with strong shades of meaning. For example, you might describe something as *wonderful* instead of *nice*, or as *tiny* instead of *small*. Read the words in the chart below. Work with your class to fill in the blank space in each row with a strong word choice. Then choose the word on each line that has the strongest shade of meaning.

	possibly	probably
large		big
happy	content	
smart		clever
unlikely	doubtful	

When writing your opinion piece, consider using words with strong shades of meaning. However, be careful to use these words accurately. To practice using different shades of meaning, choose one of the sets of three words in the chart above. Use each of the three words in a separate sentence, showing how the word could be used to connect to real-life things or events.

_____

_____

_____

_____

_____

_____

Writing Process

Now that you have read and analyzed an opinion piece, you are going to create your own by following these steps of the writing process.

1. Get Ready: Brainstorm List topics you might want to write about. Choose the topic you have the strongest opinion about.

2. Organize Use a graphic organizer to organize and plan your opinion piece.

3. Draft Create the first draft of your opinion piece.

4. Peer Review Work with a partner to evaluate and improve your draft.

5. Revise Use suggestions from your peer review to revise your opinion piece.

6. Edit Check your work carefully for spelling, punctuation, and grammar errors.

7. Publish Create a final version of your opinion piece.

Writing Assignment

In this lesson, you will write your own opinion piece. As you create this piece, remember the elements of the mentor text that expressed the writer's idea most strongly. Read the following assignment.

> Suppose that your class is going to get a class pet. What type of pet should your class choose? Why?
>
> Write three to five paragraphs telling your opinion about the type of animal that would make the best class pet. Be sure to use facts to support your opinion. Try to convince the class that your idea is the best one.

1. Get Ready: Brainstorm a Topic

The first step in writing an opinion piece is to choose your topic. Begin by listing a few possible class pets. For each one, write the best reason in favor of getting this pet and the best reason against getting this pet.

Here's how the author of the mentor opinion piece brainstormed topics.

	Zoo	Museum
reason for	We can see live animals.	We can see more animals in less time.
reason against	The animals might be hiding and we can't see them.	We'll be inside all day.

Try It!   Use a Brainstorming Graphic Organizer

Now use the chart below to help brainstorm your own opinion piece. Choose the pet for which you can make the most convincing argument.

	Pet 1: _____	Pet 2: _____	Pet 3: _____
reason for			
reason against			

Brainstorm Ideas for Your Topic

You can use a graphic organizer to help brainstorm ideas and details for your opinion piece. Here is how the author of the mentor text used the graphic organizer.

OPINION Begin by stating your opinion clearly and strongly.

REASONS Give reasons that support your opinion. You may change these reasons or add other reasons as you draft your opinion piece.

DETAILS Add one or more details for each reason. These details should be facts, not just additional opinions. You may think of more details as you draft your opinion piece.

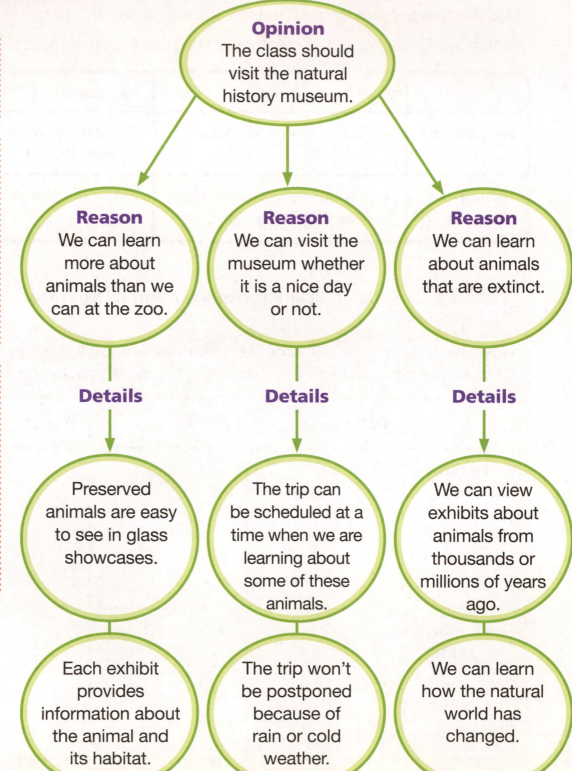

Opinion
The class should visit the natural history museum.

Reason
We can learn more about animals than we can at the zoo.

Reason
We can visit the museum whether it is a nice day or not.

Reason
We can learn about animals that are extinct.

Details

Details

Details

Preserved animals are easy to see in glass showcases.

The trip can be scheduled at a time when we are learning about some of these animals.

We can view exhibits about animals from thousands or millions of years ago.

Each exhibit provides information about the animal and its habitat.

The trip won't be postponed because of rain or cold weather.

We can learn how the natural world has changed.

Try It!

Use a Graphic Organizer for Brainstorming

Now use the graphic organizer to brainstorm your opinion, reasons, and details for your own opinion piece.

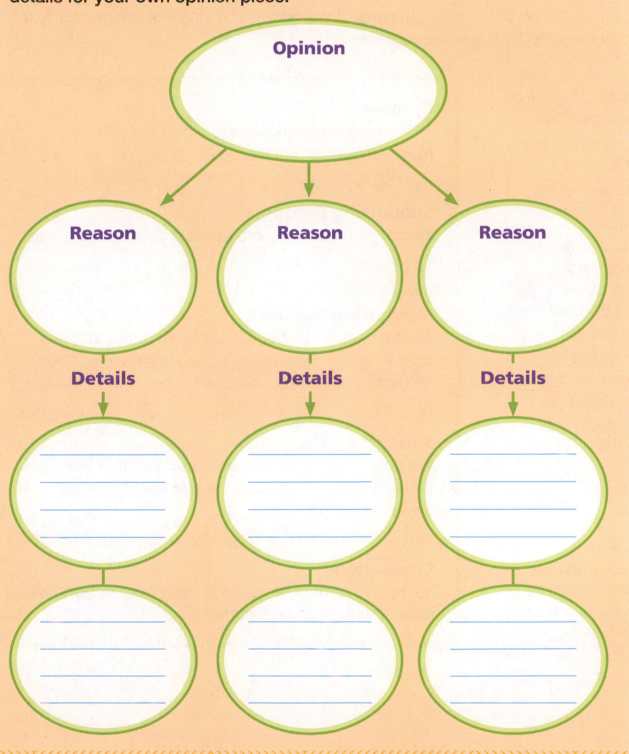

2. Organize

You are almost ready to begin a draft of your opinion piece. You can use a graphic organizer to help organize the ideas and details you gathered while brainstorming. You can then refer to the graphic organizer as you work through the different parts of your draft. The writer of the mentor text completed this graphic organizer.

INTRODUCTION In the first paragraph, you

- tell the topic of your opinion piece
- state your opinion about the topic

SUPPORTING PARAGRAPHS In the second, third, and fourth paragraphs, you

- give reasons that support your opinion
- elaborate on each reason with facts and details

CONCLUSION Your conclusion should briefly summarize your reasons and end strongly.

Opinion
The class should take a field trip to the natural history museum, not the zoo.

Supporting Reason 1
We can learn about more animals in less time at the museum.

Supporting Reason 2
Another reason is that we can learn about animals from long ago. For example, we might see exhibits on dinosaurs or saber-toothed tigers at the museum.

Supporting Reason 3
We don't need to worry about bad weather if we go to the museum. We can schedule the trip for fall, winter, or spring.

Conclusion
To make the most of our time away from school, we must visit the natural history museum.

Try It!

Organize Your Opinion Piece

Now use the graphic organizer below to organize the ideas and details you want to use in the different paragraphs of your draft.

Opinion

Supporting Reason 1

Supporting Reason 2

Supporting Reason 3

Conclusion

3. Draft

Now it is time to write the first draft of your opinion piece. Remember, your draft does not have to be perfect! This is the time to use your notes, get your ideas down in some sort of organized way, and have fun. You will have time to revise your writing later. Start by drafting your opinion piece on a computer or on a separate sheet of paper. Tell your opinion about what kind of pet your class should get. Provide several reasons that support your opinion.

Writer's Craft: Using Linking Words and Phrases

Linking words and phrases help writing flow smoothly. They also help readers understand how reasons and opinions are connected. Here are some common linking words and phrases.

Linking words	also, because, but, first, finally, however, next, since, therefore, while
Linking phrases	for example, even though, for this reason, as a result, in conclusion

The author of the mentor text uses linking words and phrases in his third paragraph.

CONNECTING IDEAS Read this section of the mentor text. Circle the linking words or phrases that connect reasons and opinions.

At both the museum and the zoo, we can learn about animals from faraway places. However, only at the museum can we see animals that have been extinct for thousands or millions of years. For example, we might see dinosaur skeletons. We also might see exhibits on woolly mammoths or saber-toothed tigers. Therefore, we can learn how the natural world has changed over time.

Try It!   Write Your First Draft

On a computer or a separate sheet of paper, create the draft of your response to the writing assignment. Remember to use linking words and phrases to connect your opinions with reasons. Use this drafting checklist to help you as you write.

✓ A good beginning gets your reader's attention. You can begin with a question, a quotation, or an interesting or funny experience.

✓ Be sure to state your opinion in the first paragraph.

✓ In each supporting paragraph, write a topic sentence that clearly states the supporting reason.

✓ Use the reasons and details you wrote during Step 2: Organize.

✓ In each supporting paragraph, include sentences with explanations, details, and facts. Use linking words and phrases to connect your reasons with your opinions.

✓ Sum up your reasons in the end. End your piece strongly so that your readers will remember your opinion.

Tips for Writing Your First Draft

• Write down key phrases and ideas before you begin writing. Sometimes this is a great warm-up to get you started.

• Focus on ideas, not details. Since you will revise and edit later, you can fix the details then. In drafting, it's the ideas that count.

• Make sure all of your ideas are connected. Use the list of linking words and phrases to help you connect your opinions with your reasons in each paragraph.

4. Peer Review

After you finish your draft, you can work with a partner to review each other's drafts. Here is a draft of the mentor text. Read it with your partner. Together, answer the questions in the boxes. Then we'll see how the writer's classmate evaluated the draft.

An Early Draft:

INTRODUCTION In his draft, the writer does not state his opinion clearly. Does he think that the class shouldn't go to either the museum or the zoo?

SUPPORTING PARAGRAPHS Both the second and third paragraphs could use some linking words. The writer could do a better job connecting his ideas. In the third paragraph, what linking word would you add to the second sentence? Why?

CONCLUSION The conclusion sums up only one of the writer's main points. How would you briefly sum up the writer's other reasons?

Our Field Trip

Why do we want to visit the museum or the zoo? Do we hope to see only some animals? At the zoo, the bears might be in caves. The seals might be underwater. The choice for the class is obvious.

At the museum, the preserved animals are all in glass showcases. Also, we can read facts about each animal in the showcases. The animals are in habitats that are painted to look exactly like their natural environment. We can learn much more about these animals' habitats than we could at the zoo.

At both the museum and the zoo, we can learn about animals from faraway regions. At the museum we can see animals from long ago. We might see dinosaur skeletons. We can learn how the natural world has changed over time.

Another reason to visit the museum is that we can plan the field trip for any time. We don't need to wait until the weather is nice in the spring. We won't have to risk postponing the trip because of rain.

In conclusion, we should visit the museum because we can see more exhibits in less time. We can learn much more in one day at the museum than we could hope to at the zoo. That is why we should visit the natural history museum.

An Example Peer Review Form

This peer review form gives an example of how a classmate evaluated the draft of the mentor text shown on the last page.

The introduction states the topic in an interesting way.	You did a good job of explaining that the choice is between visiting the museum and the zoo.
The writer gives a clear, strong opinion statement in the first paragraph.	You could improve your opinion piece by stating your opinion more clearly.
The writer supports the opinion with at least three strong reasons.	You did a good job of providing three reasons for your opinion.
The writer uses interesting details to support these reasons.	You could improve your opinion piece by supporting these reasons with more details.
The writer uses linking words and phrases to connect ideas and help the writing flow smoothly.	You did a good job of using the linking phrase "another reason" to begin paragraph 4.
	You could improve your opinion piece by adding linking words to connect ideas in paragraphs 2 and 3.
The conclusion sums up the supporting reasons and ends strongly.	You did a good job of recalling one of your earlier points.
	You could improve your opinion piece by summing up the other reasons for your opinion.

Try It!   Peer Review with a Partner

Now you are going to work with a partner to review each other's opinion piece drafts. You will use the peer review form below. If you need help, look back at the mentor text writer's peer review form for suggestions.

The introduction states the topic in an interesting way. The writer gives a clear, strong opinion statement in the first paragraph.	You did a good job of You could improve your opinion piece by
The writer supports the opinion with at least three strong reasons. The writer uses interesting details to support these reasons.	You did a good job of You could improve your opinion piece by
The writer uses linking words and phrases to connect ideas and help the writing flow smoothly.	You did a good job of You could improve your opinion piece by
The conclusion sums up the supporting reasons and ends strongly.	You did a good job of You could improve your opinion piece by

Try It! **Record Key Peer Review Comments**

Now it's time for you and your partner to share your comments with each other. Listen to your partner's feedback, and write down the key comments in the left column. Then write some ideas for improving your draft in the right column.

My review says that my introduction	I will
My review says that my first supporting reason	I will
My review says that my second supporting reason	I will
My review says that my third supporting reason	I will
My review says that my conclusion	I will

Use the space below to write anything else you notice about your draft that you think you can improve.

5. Revise

In this step of the writing process, you will work on the parts of your draft that need improvement. Use the peer review form that your classmate completed to help you. Also use your own ideas about how to improve each part of your opinion piece. This checklist includes things to think about as you revise.

Revision Checklist

✔ Does my beginning catch the reader's interest?

✔ Do I state my main idea clearly in the first paragraph?

✔ Do topic sentences clearly state the supporting reasons?

✔ Do I use explanations, details, and facts to support my opinion?

✔ Do I use linking words to connect my opinions with my reasons?

✔ Is my conclusion interesting? Have I summed up my main points well?

Writer's Craft: Using Comparatives and Superlatives

Some comparative and superlative adjectives and adverbs are formed by adding *-er* and *-est*. Others use *more* or *most*.

COMPARATIVES AND SUPERLATIVES

Adjectives and adverbs can have comparative and superlative forms to indicate *more of* or *the most of* a quality. Underline three comparatives in this paragraph. Circle three superlatives.

> At the museum, the coolest animals are all clearly placed in glass showcases and can be seen most easily. We won't have to waste the class's valuable time looking for animals that aren't even out where we can see them. Also, we can read the most interesting facts about each animal in the showcases. The bigger animals' habitats are painted, which more precisely reflects their natural environments. We can learn about these animals faster than we could at the zoo.

Try It!   Revise Your Opinion Piece

Using comparative or superlative adjectives and adverbs will help make your opinion piece more interesting and more convincing. For each of the words below, write a sentence using the word in its comparative or superlative form.

cool _____

easily _____

difficult _____

wisely _____

Writing Assignment

Now it's time to revise the draft of your opinion piece. Continue working on a computer or on a separate sheet of paper. Review the assignment, repeated below, and the checklist. Doing so will help you know that you have included everything you need.

> Suppose that your class is going to get a class pet. What type of pet should your class choose? Why?
>
> Write three to five paragraphs telling your opinion about the type of animal that would make the best class pet. Be sure to use facts to support your opinion. Try to convince the class that your idea is the best one.

6. Edit

After revising your opinion piece, you will edit it. When you edit, you read very carefully to be sure to find any mistakes in your writing. Here's a checklist of some things to look for as you edit.

Editing Checklist

- ✓ Are all of your sentences complete?
- ✓ Did you begin each sentence with a capital letter?
- ✓ Did you use capital letters for all proper nouns?
- ✓ Does each sentence end with the correct punctuation?
- ✓ Have you used commas correctly?
- ✓ Are all of your words spelled correctly?

You can use these editing marks to mark any errors you find.

^ Add	“” Add quotation marks	^ Add comma
/ Change capital letter to lowercase	Delete	˅ Add apostrophe
⊙ Add period	≡ Change lowercase letter to capital	

This paragraph from an early draft of the mentor text shows how to use editing marks.

The museum would be a better field trip than the zoo at the zoo the Bears might be hiding in caves. Wed wait for hours and finaly say, Forget it. The seals ~~seals~~ might be under the water. At the museum, we can se many more animals in less time. We should visit the natural history museum.

Language Focus: Capitalization and Punctuation

Every sentence begins with a **capital letter** and ends with a **punctuation mark**, such as a period or question mark. However, capital letters and punctuation marks are often used in the middle of sentences as well. We use capital letters for proper nouns, such as people's names. We use commas between separate parts of a sentence.

Quoting Dialogue

Use quotation marks around the words that people speak in the text. Place a comma inside the end quotation marks if your sentence continues beyond the dialogue.

Example: "We want Chinese food," the kids said.

Apostrophes

The apostrophe has multiple purposes. Some apostrophes indicate possession. Others replace missing letters in contractions, such as *shouldn't* or *you're*.

Forming Possessives

Add an apostrophe and an *s* at the end of singular nouns to form the possessive (showing ownership or possession).

For plural nouns, place the apostrophe after the *s* that ends the word. Do not add an additional *s*.

Examples: Ruth's bicycle, Chris's goldfish, many lions' coats

At the museum, the coolest animals are all clearly placed in glass showcases and can be seen most easily. We won't have to waste the class's valuable time looking for animals that aren't even out where we can see them. Also, we can read the most interesting facts about each animal in the showcases. The bigger animals' habitats are painted, which shows their natural environment. We can learn faster about these animals than we could at the zoo.

APOSTROPHES Read this section of the mentor text. Circle each place where an apostrophe is used to form a possessive. Draw a star next to each place where an apostrophe is used in a contraction.

Try It! Language and Editing Practice

Use what you have learned about capitalization and punctuation, and underline the correct version of each sentence below.

My favorite book is *Alice's Adventures in Wonderland*.

My favorite book is *Alices Adventures in Wonderland*.

"Let's go over to Mike's house" I said.

"Let's go over to Mike's house," I said.

The *Mayflower* landed in Plymouth. Massachusetts

The *Mayflower* landed in Plymouth, Massachusetts.

Now use editing marks to correct the errors in these paragraphs.

"We shoud get an iguana said Max. "I saw one at the zoo in San Diego. It was really cool!

That's just a big lizard said Maya. I don't like reptiles she told us.

I said let's get a rabbit for the class. Sarahs family has a rabbit and it is really cute.

The class agreed. then we read a story called "My Pet Bunny" The story taught us how to take care of rabbits.

Try It!

Edit Your Opinion Piece

Now edit your opinion piece. Use this checklist and the editing marks you have learned to correct any errors you find.

☐ Are all of your sentences complete?

☐ Did you begin each sentence with a capital letter?

☐ Did you use capital letters for all proper nouns?

☐ Does each sentence end with the correct punctuation?

☐ Have you used commas correctly?

☐ Are all of your words spelled correctly?

Editing Tips

- Read your writing aloud. This will help you discover missing words and awkward phrases. Ask yourself, "Does that sound right?"

- As you read, listen carefully for stops and pauses. These are places where punctuation often goes. Ask yourself if you are missing any punctuation.

- Read your opinion piece over at a slow pace at least two times. When reading for small details, one reading is not enough.

7. Publish

On a computer or a separate sheet of paper, create a neat final draft of your opinion piece. Correct all errors that you identified while editing your draft. Be sure to give your opinion piece an interesting title.

The final step is to publish your opinion piece. Here are some different ways you might choose to share your work.

- Read aloud your opinion piece to your class or to a small group of your classmates. See if you can convince them of your opinion.

- Share your opinion piece with others who have written about the same animal. Vote to decide which opinion piece is the most convincing.

- Use your opinion piece to create a newspaper editorial.

- Create a poster using your opinion piece and drawings or photographs from magazines or newspapers.

Technology Suggestions

- Upload your opinion piece onto your class or school blog.
- Find images on the Internet of the type of pet you have chosen, and use them to illustrate your work.

Writing Handbook

A Guide to Functional Texts

Functional texts are things you read and write to help you in your day-to-day life. If you need to cook something, you read the recipe first. If you are going to a special event, you read the invitation to find out when and where the event will be. If you plan a party, you write invitations with the details. In this section, you will find examples of different functional texts and labels that show you the important features of each text. If you are asked to read or write one of these functional texts, use the sample in this handbook as a model to follow.

On the top left-hand corner of the envelope, write your name, street address, city, state, and zip code.

Put a stamp on the top right-hand corner of the envelope.

Sender's name
Street Address
City, State Zip code

In the middle of the envelope, write the recipient's name, street address, city, state, and zip code.

Recipient's Name
Street Address
City, State Zip code

Megan Pickens
111 Broad Street
Merchantville, FL 12345

Dylan Thompson
22 Ranch Road
Plainville, Texas 45678

Write your address at the top of the letter. Include the date.

12 Hastings Road
Juneau, Alaska 99801
October 14, 2012

Address the person you are writing to with a standard greeting.

Dear Fred,

What's up? It was so great to visit you in Nebraska. I can't wait until next summer when you come to Alaska. My mom promised that she would take us on long hikes and even let us camp in a tent outside. I told my best friend Jaime that you would be coming. He is really excited to meet you. He's never met anyone from Nebraska before.

The body paragraphs of your letter should be well organized and clear.

Remember that night when we stayed up almost all night playing video games? We were trying to beat the last level of MindBusters II. Well, I finally beat it! It was a little tricky, and took me a couple of hours. I am sure you'll figure it out soon, if you haven't already.

Remember to maintain a friendly tone in your letter.

OK, I have to go and help my mom shovel snow. Can you believe we already have snow? We still have school though. We don't get many snow days. See you next summer!

Your closing should say good-bye.

Your friend,

Sam

Sam

Sign your letter.

Address the person you are writing to with a standard greeting such as "Dear."

Dear Ms. Osterberg,

The body paragraphs of your letter should be well organized and clear.

Please excuse Eli from school for the rest of this week. He has come down with the flu, and his doctor has suggested he stay home and rest. I expect that he will make up any and all of the assignments he is missing. I will come to school tomorrow to pick up some work and books for him. Thank you.

The note should be short and have a clear focus.

Sincerely,

Jason Lee

Jason Lee

Your closing should match the tone of the rest of the letter. "With thanks" and "Best" are good choices.

Sign your note.

Start by giving the reason for the event.

Elizabeth Novak is celebrating her tenth birthday!

* 10 *

Join us as we celebrate on
Saturday, May 19, 2012 at 2:00 p.m.

Moonlight Roller Rink
111 Winters Street
Millersburg, Ohio

Regrets only to Mr. and Mrs. Novak (123) 456-7890.

Include the date and time of the event.

Provide the location's name and address.

Provide a way for your guests to respond to the invitation.

Include a title that describes what is shown.

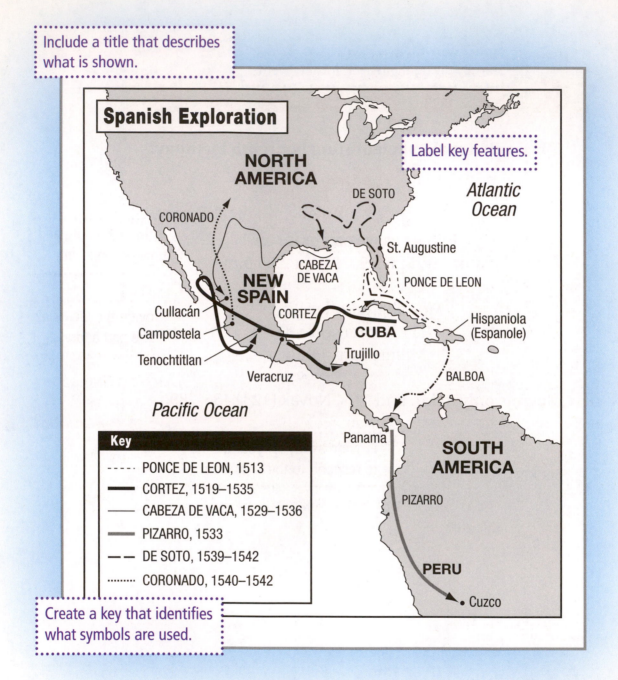

Spanish Exploration

NORTH AMERICA

DE SOTO

Atlantic Ocean

CORONADO

St. Augustine

CABEZA DE VACA

PONCE DE LEON

NEW SPAIN

Cullacán

CORTEZ

Campostela

CUBA

Hispaniola (Espanole)

Tenochtitlan

Trujillo

Veracruz

BALBOA

Pacific Ocean

Panama

SOUTH AMERICA

PIZARRO

PERU

Cuzco

Label key features.

Key
- - - - - PONCE DE LEON, 1513
━━━ CORTEZ, 1519–1535
─── CABEZA DE VACA, 1529–1536
━━ PIZARRO, 1533
– – DE SOTO, 1539–1542
······· CORONADO, 1540–1542

Create a key that identifies what symbols are used.

Fall Cake

Ingredients:

- 1 sponge cake
- 1 can of white frosting
- 1 package of mixed-color candies
- 1 small jar of cherries

Instructions:

1. Place the cake on a plate.

2. Open the frosting can. Spread the frosting over the sponge cake with a knife or spoon.

3. Open the package of candies. Pick out candies of different colors. Use them to spell FALL on top of the frosting.

4. Place the cherries all around the edge of the cake.

5. Enjoy!

Write a title for the procedure.

Making a Drum

If you like to make music, this is a good project for you. Follow these simple steps to make a drum.

Things you need:

- An empty round oatmeal container
- Some string or yarn
- 2 pencils
- 2 spools
- Construction paper
- Glue
- Markers

List all the items needed.

Look at the list of things you need to make a drum. Are these things you can find easily?

Steps:

Procedure steps should be numbered.

1. First, draw a design on the construction paper using the markers.
2. Cover the oatmeal box with the decorated paper.
3. Poke a hole in the center of the top of the container.
4. Poke another hole in the center of the bottom of the container.
5. Thread yarn through both holes. Cut the yarn so that it is long enough for the drum to hang safely around your neck.
6. To make drumsticks, put the spools on the pencils. Glue them so that they stay in place.
7. Finally, play your drum.

Instructions should be written clearly. Be sure they explain exactly what steps must be done and how to complete them.

Write a title for the experiment.

Weathering

When wind blows, it carries sand. The sand rubs some of the rock away. When rain falls, it slowly washes away some of the rock. When ice forms on a rock, it can break off pieces of the rock. This is called weathering. Weathering eats away at rocks. You can do an experiment to show how weathering works.

Materials:

List all the materials needed for the experiment.

An uncooked egg

Vinegar

Steps:

Steps should be numbered.

1. Get a glass. The glass must be tall enough to hold the egg and some vinegar.

2. Be careful. Put the egg in the glass.

3. Pour vinegar in the glass. Add enough vinegar to make the egg float.

4. Let the egg sit for one day.

5. Look for bubbles. Bubbles mean the vinegar is eating away the shell.

6. Keep the egg in the vinegar for one week. After this time, the shell will be gone. The egg will be whole. It will look like an egg with a clear shell.

7. Take the egg out of the vinegar. It will be soft, like a water balloon. Don't squeeze it, or it will pop!

Vinegar is like rain with chemicals in it. It wears away the egg's tough shell. It weathers the shell the way rain and wind weather a rock.

Instructions should be written clearly. Be sure they explain exactly how to perform the experiment and do not contain unnecessary information.

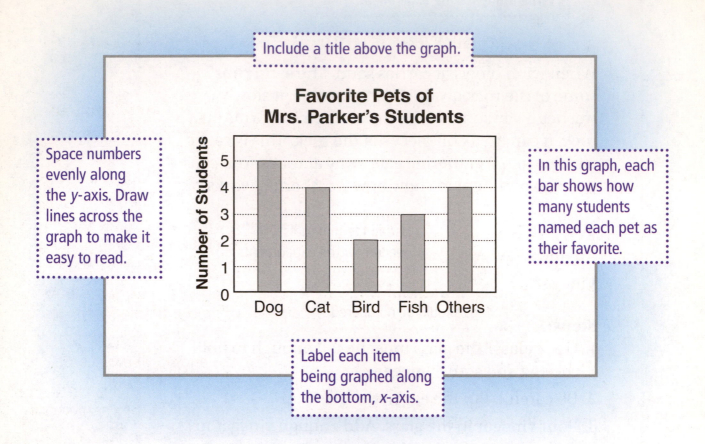

Include a title above the graph.

Favorite Pets of Mrs. Parker's Students

Space numbers evenly along the *y*-axis. Draw lines across the graph to make it easy to read.

In this graph, each bar shows how many students named each pet as their favorite.

Label each item being graphed along the bottom, *x*-axis.

Glossary

apostrophe (') a punctuation mark that shows possession or takes the place of missing letters in a contraction (Lessons 5, 11)

ask and answer questions to ask questions about key details in a passage and use the text to find the answers (Lessons 1, 2, 4, 6, 7, 8, 10)

author's purpose the reason why an author writes a text, usually to inform, entertain, or persuade the reader (Lesson 4)

body the middle section of a piece of writing (Lesson 9)

capitalization the use of capital, or uppercase, letters (Lesson 11)

caption a phrase or sentence that tells what a photograph or illustration is about (Lesson 10)

cause a reason why something happens (Lessons 8, 10)

cause and effect the relationship that shows how one event causes another event to happen (Lessons 8, 10)

chapter a section of a story (Lesson 2)

character a person, animal, or other creature in a story or poem (Lessons 1, 2, 3, 6)

character traits details about a character's physical appearance or personality (Lessons 2, 6)

climax the turning point of a story; usually the most exciting part (Lesson 2)

comma (,) a punctuation mark that shows a pause in a sentence, a date, or an address (Lessons 5, 9)

comparative adjective an adjective that compares two things using the ending -er or the word more (Lesson 11)

comparative adverb an adverb that compares two actions using the ending -er or the word more (Lesson 11)

compare to tell how things are alike (Lessons 2, 4)

complex sentence a sentence that includes a main clause and one or more subordinate clauses (Lesson 9)

compound sentence a sentence that contains two or more simple sentences, or main clauses (Lesson 9)

conclusion the ending of a piece of writing (Lessons 3, 5, 9, 11)

conflict a problem that the characters in a story must solve (Lessons 2, 3)

context clues the words or phrases around an unfamiliar word that help you understand its meaning (Lessons 1, 2, 3, 4, 6, 7, 8, 10)

contrast to tell how things are different (Lesson 4)

coordinating conjunction a word, such as and, or, or but, that joins main clauses in a sentence (Lesson 9)

description colorful words and phrases that paint a picture in a reader's mind (Lessons 3, 7)

details information in a fictional or personal narrative that tells who, what, when, where, or how (Lessons 1, 3, 5)

dialogue words that are spoken by characters in a story or play (Lessons 2, 3, 5, 6)

dictionary a book in which words are listed alphabetically with their meanings, pronunciations, and other information (Lesson 9)

drama a story that is performed on a stage by actors; a play (Lesson 6)

effect a result of a cause (Lessons 8, 10)

fable a made-up story that teaches a lesson (Lesson 1)

fictional narrative a story that is made up by a writer (Lesson 3)

glossary an alphabetical list of difficult words or technical terms and their meanings; found at the end of a book (Lesson 9)

heading a word or phrase above a section of text that tells what it is about (Lessons 4, 8, 10)

historical nonfiction text that tells about real events or people from the past (Lesson 4)

illustration a picture that shows information to help you understand a story (Lessons 1, 2)

informative/explantory text writing that provides facts and details about a nonfiction topic (Lesson 9)

introduction the beginning of a piece of writing, which often tells the main idea (Lessons 9, 11)

label a word or phrase that names something in a photograph, map, or diagram (Lessons 8, 10)

linking words and phrases words and phrases that connect ideas to make writing flow smoothly (Lessons 9, 11)

main idea the most important idea in a piece of writing (Lessons 4, 9, 10)

make inferences to use details from a text, along with personal knowledge and experience, to figure out something that is not directly stated by the author (Lessons 2, 6)

map a drawing or picture of an area of land or water that shows selected features (Lessons 8, 10)

moral a short lesson about life (Lesson 1)

motivation the reason a character does something (Lessons 2, 6)

myth a story that tells how something in nature came to be (Lesson 1)

nonliteral language words and phrases that mean something other than their usual dictionary meanings (Lessons 2, 6, 7, 9)

noun a word that names a person, place, thing, or idea (Lesson 3)

opinion a personal belief that cannot be proven true (Lesson 11)

opinion piece a type of writing in which the author states a personal belief and tries to persuade others to agree (Lesson 11)

period (.) a punctuation mark used at the end of a statement (Lesson 11)

personal narrative a type of writing in which the author describes a personal experience (Lesson 5)

plot the series of events in a story (Lesson 2)

poetry literature written in lines and stanzas; often uses rhyme, rhythm, and colorful descriptions (Lesson 7)

point of view the perspective from which a story is told (Lessons 1, 6)

possessive a word form that shows ownership (Lessons 5, 11)

prefix a group of letters added to the beginning of a word that changes its meaning (Lesson 5)

pronoun a word that takes the place of a noun (Lesson 3)

question mark (?) a punctuation mark used at the end of a question (Lesson 11)

quotation marks (" ") punctuation marks used to show the exact words of a speaker (Lessons 5, 11)

repetition the repeating of a word, phrase, or line in a poem (Lesson 7)

research to gather information from sources such as books, Web sites, and newspapers (Lesson 9)

resolution the conclusion of a story during which the problem is solved (Lesson 2)

resource material in print or online that provides information on a topic and is used for research (Lesson 9)

retell to tell a story again in your own words (Lesson 1)

rhyme the repeating of sounds at the ends of lines of poetry (Lesson 7)

rhythm the beat, or pattern of stressed and unstressed syllables, in a line of poetry (Lesson 7)

root word the base, or main part, of a word (Lesson 5)

scene a section of a drama (Lesson 6)

scientific nonfiction writing that provides factual information about a science topic (Lesson 10)

sensory language words that appeal to the five senses: sight, hearing, taste, smell, and touch (Lesson 5)

sequence the order in which events happen (Lessons 2, 3, 6, 10)

setting where and when a story takes place (Lesson 2)

short story a made-up story that is usually only a few pages long (Lesson 2)

simple sentence a sentence that has a subject and a predicate and states a complete thought (Lesson 9)

spelling the correct order of letters in a word (Lesson 5)

stage directions instructions in a play that tell the actors what to do (Lesson 6)

stanza a group of lines in a poem (Lesson 7)

steps in a process a type of text organization in which the writer presents the stages of doing something (Lesson 8)

subject-verb agreement when the subject and verb in a sentence match in number as singular or plural (Lesson 3)

subordinate clause a group of words that has a subject and predicate but does not stand alone as a sentence (Lesson 9)

subordinating conjunction a word, such as *although, since,* or *because,* that introduces a subordinate clause in a sentence (Lesson 9)

superlative adjective an adjective that compares more than two things using the ending *-est* or the word *most* (Lesson 11)

superlative adverb an adverb that compares more than two actions using the ending *-est* or the word *most* (Lesson 11)

supporting details facts, examples, or other information in a passage that back up, or support, the main idea; in writing, facts and examples that support the topic of the composition (Lessons 4, 9, 10, 11)

supporting paragraphs paragraphs in a text that elaborate on a topic with explanations, supporting details, and facts (Lessons 9, 11)

supporting reasons facts, examples, or other information that a writer gives to support his or her opinion (Lesson 11)

technical text writing that explains how to do something or how something works (Lesson 8)

text feature an element, such as a title or heading, that helps readers find information (Lessons 4, 9)

theme a message or truth about life (Lessons 1, 2)

time-order language words and phrases, such as *first*, *next*, and *finally*, that tell the order of events (Lessons 3, 5)

title the name of a piece of writing (Lesson 4)

verb a word that shows action or state of being (Lesson 3)

Acknowledgments

Picture Credits 5, 16 (t), 16 (b), 37, 62, 65, 67, 70, 74, 81, 103, 104–109 (bg), 112–116 (bg), 119, 128–129, 130, 133, 135, 136–137, 136 (t), 140 (t), 140 (b), 141, 142, 143 (t), 143 (b), 144 (b), 147, 150, 173, 174, 176, 180, 182, 183, 187, 189, 198 (b) Thinkstock; 19 Flickr; 39, 40, 79, 82, 126–127, 134, 136–137 (b), 144 (t), 181, 184, 190 Shutterstock; 61, 63, 64, 70–71, 74, 76 Library of Congress; 66 National Archives; 72 (t), 73 Wikimedia Commons; 72 (b)Wikipedia; 177 NOAA.

Illustrations Cover Jennifer Kalis; 6–7 Francesca Dafne; 8–9 Monica Armino; 12–15 Katriona Chapman; 20–25 Joanne Renaud; 28–34 Dani Jones; 74 Jeff Crosby; 105–109 Andy Catling; 112–116 Colleen Madden; 120–123 Karen Donnely; 142, 149, 156, 175, 180 Q2AMedia.